International Conference on Innovation in Engineering and Vocational Education (ICIEVE 2018)

MATEC Web of Conferences Volume 205 (2018)

Bandung, Indonesia
25-26 August 2018

Editors:

Yuli Utanto

ISBN: 978-1-5108-7119-9

Printed from e-media with permission by:

Curran Associates, Inc.
57 Morehouse Lane
Red Hook, NY 12571

Some format issues inherent in the e-media version may also appear in this print version.

Printed by Curran Associates, Inc. (2018)

For additional information, please contact EDP Sciences – Web of Conferences
at the address below.

EDP Sciences – Web of Conferences
17, Avenue du Hoggar
Parc d'Activité de Courtabœuf
BP 112
F-91944 Les Ulis Cedex A
France

Phone: +33 (0) 1 69 18 75 75
Fax: +33 (0) 1 69 28 84 91

contact-edps@webofconferences.org

Additional copies of this publication are available from:

Curran Associates, Inc.
57 Morehouse Lane
Red Hook, NY 12571 USA
Phone: 845-758-0400
Fax: 845-758-2633
Email: curran@proceedings.com
Web: www.proceedings.com

TABLE OF CONTENTS

Preface

The 3rd ICIEVE 2018, the International Conference on Innovation in Engineering and Vocational Education, held on August 25-26, 2018 at Aryaduta Hotel, Indonesia. The conference was a platform for scientists, scholars, engineers, industrial professionals, and researchers to exchange, share, and discuss their innovation, experiences, research works and problem solving techniques in all issues in engineering and vocational education.

The participants of ICIEVE 2018 were from around the world with a variety of background, including academics, industry, and even well-known enterprise. In general, there were papers discussing such various topics as engineering and technology innovation (mechanical engineering, chemical engineering, civil engineering, etc.), engineering education (basic science in engineering education, engineering education reforms, new technologies in education, etc.), and vocational education and training (industry-driven training programs and collaborations, lifelong learning – reskilling and upskilling, government and policy, etc.). We would like to thank all of those who helped and supported ICIEVE 2018. Each individual and institution's support was very important for the success of this conference. Specifically, we would like to acknowledge the advisory board, scientific committee, and organizing committee for their valuable advice, help, suggestions, and support in the organization and helpful peerreviewing process of the papers.

We would also extend our best gratitude to keynote speakers for their valuable contribution for sharing ideas and knowledge in the ICIEVE 2018. We sincerely hope that ICIEVE 2018 will be a forum for excellent discussions for improving the quality of research and development in relation to innovation in engineering and vocational education. We also hope that this forum will put forward new ideas and promote collaborative researches among participants. We believe that the proceedings can serve as an important research source of reference and the knowledge. Indeed, the proceedings will lead to not only scientific and engineering progress but also other new products and processes for better science and technology in vocational education.

The Editor

Statement of Peer review

In submitting conference proceedings to *Web of Conferences*, the editors of the proceedings certify to the Publisher that

1. They adhere to its **Policy on Publishing Integrity** in order to safeguard good scientific practice in publishing.
2. All articles have been subjected to peer review administered by the proceedings editors.
3. Reviews have been conducted by expert referees, who have been requested to provide unbiased and constructive comments aimed, whenever possible, at improving the work.
4. Proceedings editors have taken all reasonable steps to ensure the quality of the materials they publish and their decision to accept or reject a paper for publication has been based only on the merits of the work and the relevance to the journal.

International Conference on Innovation in Engineering and Vocational Education (Bandung, Indonesia, 25 – 26 August, 2018

Proceedings editor(s): Yuli Utanto

Date and editor's signature 31 August 2018

17, avenue du Hoggar - PA de Courtabœuf – BP 112 - 91944 Les Ulis Cedex A (France)
Tél. : 33 (0)1 69 18 75 75 - Fax : 33(0)1 69 07 45 17 – www.edpsciences.org

The Role of YouTube Media as a Means to Optimize Early Childhood Cognitive Development

Dwi Asmiarti[1] and *Guntur Winangun*[2]

[1]Universitas Negeri Semarang, Indonesia

[2]Universitas PGRI Semarang, Indonesia

Abstract. Early childhood cognitive development is formed faster in the first four years of life. YouTube as a video-based application media is used as a means to optimize children's cognitive development by some parents. The objective of this study was to determine the role of YouTube media in optimizing cognitive development in early childhood. The method used is qualitative with a phenomenological approach. Data collection techniques in this study were interviews and observations to parents of YouTube media users as a means of optimizing a more optimal development in aspects of imagination, language, curiosity, and concentration. Thus it can be concluded that YouTube media can be used as a means to optimize cognitive development in early childhood.

Keywords: early childhood, YouTube media, cognitive development

1 Introduction

Children's cognitive development shows the development of children's thinking. Cognitive development is the basis of a child's ability to think. This is appropriate with the opinion of Ahmad Susanto (2011: 48) that cognitive is a process of thinking, namely the ability of individuals to connect, assess, and consider an event. So cognitive processes are related to the level of intelligence that marks a person with various interests, especially aimed at learning ideas. Cognitive development has an important role for success children in learning because some activities in learning are always related to thinking problems.

Cognitive development is an emerging and rapidly developing aspect of the first four years of life. At this age, there will be many parts of the brain cortex that produce excess synapses as an initial implication of the child's development of interacting with the surrounding environment (Berk, 2012). Early age so-called golden age because of the physical and motor development of children thrive and grow rapidly both the development of emotional, intellectual, moral and even language character. For that, as parents, we should be able to provide the appropriate stimulation to help the development of cognitive children and not to miss the golden age passed by. There are factors that influence this development. Factors that influence cognitive development according to Piaget in Siti Partini (2003: 4) that "experiences derived from the environment and maturity both influence children's cognitive development". Meanwhile, according to Soemiarti and Patmonodewo (2003: 20), cognitive development is influenced by the growth of brain cells and the development of relationships between brain cells. The health and nutrition conditions of the child although still in the mother's womb will affect the growth and development of the child. According to Piaget in Asri Budiningsih (2005: 35) the more a person ages, the more complex his nerve cells are and the more he is able to improve. When an individual develops to maturity will experience a biological adaptation to the environment that will lead to qualitative changes in cognitive structure. There is another opinion that states that many factors can influence cognitive development. According to Ahmad Susanto (2011: 59-60) factors that can influence cognitive development such as: factors of heredity or descent, environmental, maturity, formation, interest and freedom.

YouTube is a service from Google that facilitates its users to upload videos and can be accessed by other users around the world for free. The availability of diverse video content also specifically for children, makes researchers interested in researching how the impact of YouTube media on children's intelligence related to the phenomenon of parents who provide video shows from YouTube to optimize cognitive development for their children.

As an important note, the most fundamental thing when discussing early childhood development cannot be separated from the role of parents. In this study, parents have a very decisive role in optimizing the effectiveness of using YouTube media in optimizing early childhood cognitive development.

2 Basic Theory

2.1. *Cognitive Development*

According to Ernawulan Syaodih and Mubair Agustin (2008: 20), cognitive development concerns the development of thinking and how thinking activities work. In his life, maybe children are faced with problems that require solutions. Resolving a problem is a more complex step self-child. Before the child is able to solve the problem the child needs to have the ability to find a solution. Husdarta and Nurlan (2010: 169) argue that development Cognitive is a continuous process, but the results are not connection (continuation) of the results previously achieved. These results differ qualitatively between one and the other. Children will pass through stages of cognitive development or period of development. Every period of development, the child tries to find a balance between cognitive structure and experiences new. Imbalance requires new accommodation as well as the transformation of the next period. Based on some of the opinions above it was concluded that the factors cognitive have an important role for children's success in learning because most of the activities in learning are always related to the problem of remembering and thinking. Cognitive development is intended so children are able to explore the surrounding world through his five senses so that with the knowledge he got the child can live his life.

Piaget in Allen (2010: 29) states that cognitive development is a process of ongoing interaction between children and their perceptual views of an object or event in an environment. Cognitive development theory is developed by Jean Piaget, a Switzerland psychologist who lives in the years 1896 - 1980. The theory provides many key concepts in the field developmental psychology and influences the development of the concept intelligence, which for Piaget, means the ability to more accurately represent the world and perform logical operations in concept representations based on reality. This theory discusses the emergence and acquisition schemata the scheme of how a person perceives his environment in the stages of development when someone acquires a new way of representing information mentally. This theory is classified into constructivism, which means, unlike theory nativism (which describes cognitive development as the appearance of innate knowledge and abilities), this theory argues that we build our cognitive abilities through motivated actions by itself to the environment. For the development of this theory, Piaget obtained the Erasmus Prize. Piaget divided the scheme used child to understand the world through four main periods that are correlated and increasingly sophisticated as growth increases age : Sensorimotor period (age 0-2 years) , preoperational period (age 2-7 years) , concrete operational period (age 7-11 years) and formal operational period (age 11 years to adult) .

2.2 YouTube Media

Basically, youtube is a website which facilitates users to share videos they have or limited to enjoying various video clips uploaded by various parties. There are various kinds of videos that can be uploaded to this site, such as music video clips from certain musicians, short films, television films, movie trailers, educational videos, vlogger video blogs, various video tutorials, and many more.

YouTube itself was established in February 2005. Youtube headquarters is in San Bruno, California, the United States initiated by three Youtube founders, namely Chad Hurley, Steven Chen, and Jawed Karim. The website which now contains billions of videos is growing very rapidly from the first time it was founded. In 2006 in November, even Google bought Youtube at a price of US $ 1.65 billion.

YouTube earns income from advertisements displayed before youtube videos are played. The ad is named with Google AdSense, a program that offers payments based on the frequency level of a video played. In February 2017, it was noted that there were videos with a total duration of 400 hours uploaded on Youtube every minute and a total of one billion hours of Youtube content watched by people every day.

2.3 Early Childhood

Hurlock (Desmita: 2013) explains that childhood begins after a dependent baby, that is, around the age of 2 years until the child is sexually mature, ie 13 years old for women and 14 years for men. Early childhood is a child aged 0-8 years. According to Beichler and Snowman (Dwi Yulianti, 2010: 7), early childhood is children between 3-6 years old. Where as the nature of early childhood (Augusta, 2012) is a unique individual where he has a pattern growth and development in physical, cognitive, socio-emotional aspects, creativity, language and special communication that are in accordance with the stages that are being passed by the child. From the various definition, researchers conclude that early childhood is a child aged 0-8 years who are in the stage of growth and development, both physical and mental. Early childhood is often referred to as the " golden age ". At this time almost all of the potential children experience sensitive times to grow and develop quickly and superbly. The development of each child is not the same because every individual has different developments. Nutritious and balanced food and intensive stimulation are needed for growth and these developments. If the child is given intensive stimulation from the environment, the child will be able to carry out the task of good development.

3 Research Methods

3.1 Research Approach

The method used in this research is qualitative research with short or phenomenology. Sugiyono (2010:14) states that qualitative research methods are often referred to as naturalistic methods because their research is carried out under natural conditions (natural setting) is also called the ethnographic method because it is on initially this method was more widely used for research in the field of cultural anthropology. The term phenomenology is often used as a general assumption to refer to subjective experiences of various types and types of subjects encountered. (Moleong, 2009: 15).

3.2 Research Focus

This study focused on how cognitive development in early childhood is stimulated using YouTube media by parents.

3.3 Research Subjects

The first subject was named Syafa Azika M aihusnah, 3 years old, the address is in the Tanggel Village, Winong District, Pati regency. The second subject was Velly Arlita Ahmad aged 2.5 years, the home address of Winong Village, Winong District, Pati regency, and the third subject was Arra, 2 years old, address of Tanggel Village, Winong District, Pati Regency.

3.4 Data Collection

Data collection methods carried out in this study were by interview and observation. The type of interview used is an unstandardized interview. Satori (2007) explains that open interviews are free interviews where researchers use interview guidelines in a formal context to collect data. While the observation used is non-participant observation. According to Sugiyono (2011), non-participant observation is an observation in conducting research researchers are not involved and only as independent observers.

3.5 Data Analysis Technique

The data analysis technique used in this study is a descriptor that contains a systematic and factual description. According to Moleong (2007), this analysis is carried out in three ways, namely: a). Data reduction, namely the process of selection, concentration, research through a rigorous selection of the focus studied, b). Exposure or data presentation, namely the process of formulating complex formations in a systematic form so that they become more simple and selective and can be understood by their meaning, c). Conclusions, namely: the last step the researcher carried out in analyzing the data continuously both at the time of data collection or after data collection.

4 Results And Discussion

4.1 Research Result

Following is the data table used in the study:

Tabel 1 data table used in the study

No	Aspects	Subject 1	Subject 2	Subject 3
1	Parents's Name	Sukaisih	Ita	Lia
2	Parents's Occupation	Kindergarten teacher	Kindergarten teacher	Private Employees
3	Name	Syafa	Velly	Arra
4	Age	3 tahun	2,5 tahun	2 tahun
5	First time stimulated by Youtube	1,5 tahun	± 2 tahun	±1 tahun
6	Video given	Children's song (gundul-gundul pacul, aku anak indonesia, dsb), kartun jalan sesama dan *Happy holiday*	Cartoon (Marsha, Larva), Children's song (abc song, 123 dan English song: *one and one*)	Introduction to colours, alphabet and hijaiyah letter, prayer, anak kreatif mandiri, cartoon (ayam, oscar, Larva, Frozen)
7	Cognitive Development	Language Imagination Consentration Curiousity	Language Imagination Consentration Curiousity	Language Imagination Consentration Curiousity
8	Video giving intensity	Rarely (depends on parents) Rarely (substitute when parents are tired of playing with children)	Rarely (When a child has no friends)	Rarely (alternate when parents are tired of playing with children)
9	Parental Assisstance	Accompanying children when watching a video then assossiate the contents of the video with the environment	Accompanying children only when watching You Tube videos online	Accompany the child every watch

4.2 Child Development

4.2.1 Language

From the results of interviews and observations that have been made, found the development of language in children, as follows:

In subject 1 parents stated that in their 2 years old children are able to do two-way communication with other people, children also master some English words like " how do you do " and some numbers in English. The child also memorizes some traditional song such as Gundul-gundul Pacul and Indonesian children's songs.

In subject 2 children can say a few words in English such as words: eyes and colours.

In subjects 3 children are able to recognize colors, some letters of the alphabet and letters hijaiyah, memorize the prayers of starting to eat, after eating, going to sleep and waking up, children can begin to imitate what is seen and heard.

4.2.2 Imagination

From the results of interviews and observations that have been made, found the development of children's imagination as follows:

In subject 1, imagination develops well. She can think of himself as a figure of the cartoon he watches, she considers the strokes she makes as perfect images. Children can imagine using a pencil like a plane that is flying, the seat is like a car, the tablecloth is used to play baronsai.

In subject 2, the child's imagination develops quite well. Children chat with dolls. She considers inanimate things as if life has feelings.

In subject 3, the child's imagination develops quite well. The child wants to be like Frozen. He also draws people who are likened to her father, mother, and brother. Children imagine making milk by stirring empty glasses.

4.2.3 Curiosity

From the results of interviews and observations that have been made, found the development of Curiosity in children.

In subject 1, when the child watches the video she always asks. Like when Tantan is sad, she asks his mother "Mommy, why is Tantan crying?", When Bob wrote the train, he asked, "What writing is it, Mrs.?", The child often asks about the surrounding objects that are similar to what he saw in the video.

In subject 2, curiosity is not much different from the subject 1. The curiosity of a child is dominated by referring only to what he watches. Like "Why can Marsha get sick?", "Where do you take the train?"

In subject 3 the child's curiosity cannot be suppressed, in contrast to the first and second subjects, which have not led to curiosity.

4.2.4 Concentration

From the results of interviews and observations that have been made, the concentration of 1,2,3 subjects is relatively the same. Her concentration is seen when the child is watching videos online on mobile phones, he is focused on what he is doing.

4.2.5 The Role of Parents

In Subject 1, parents play an active role in accompanying children when watching a video and then linking the contents of the video to the environment. In the sense of implementing content with what is around and experienced by children. Parents also give colored books and show the colors in the video. In the street cartoon show, fellow parents gave examples of moral values in cartoon characters.

In subject 2, parents only play an active role when children watch YouTube videos, when in online mode. Sometimes children are left watching alone specifically on videos that have been downloaded by themselves and chosen by parents.

In subject 3, parents play an active role in accompanying children when watching YouTube videos. In this case, YouTube videos are only used by parents as a substitute for learning to help children's learning when parents are troubled or tired.

4.3 Discussion

Based on the comparison of the subjects the results of the study explained that the children of the three subjects showed cognitive development in the area of imagination, language, curiosity, and concentration. Referring to the tables of YouTube video shows given from the three subjects included in the category of cartoons and music for children.

The most prominent and rapidly growing in YouTube video stimulation for the three subjects are in terms of language and imagination. This relates to the age of the three subjects who are in the stage of imitating the environment so that the stimulation of YouTube videos is based on English, songs, and prayer can be recorded by children in their memory well. From subjects 1 and 2 indicate a developmental tendency for color recognition. So in line with Kuriniawati's findings (2013) that audiovisual stimulation of video is able to help optimize cognitive development in color recognition more effectively in early childhood. While the findings in the child's imagination area, the interesting thing is the way children interpret their environment according to the imagination of what is contained in the video given. This concept is the same as the development of egocentrism in children which is marked by perceiving the outside world according to their will. Child behavior that is active here can be said to be the potential for kinesthetic intelligence that will develop in the child.

Furthermore, regarding the role of parents in providing stimulation, all three have a rare intensity and can assist in the stimulation process for each of their children. This implies that video stimulation is not the main thing given by parents to help optimize children's cognitive development. Parents of the three subjects stated that gadget, especially for video, is not the only stimulation that parents take preventively. This is to prevent addiction or the negative impact of using gadget. Parents also provide plenty of space for children to socialize with peers so that they can explore the environment.

Conclusion

In this study, it can be concluded that stimulation with YouTube videos can be used as a means to optimize early childhood cognitive development. This finding basically correlates audio-visual based learning in schools by recognizing media objects with YouTube. The results of the study illustrate that children who are given stimulation have a similar effect to previous studies. This can be a contributing method for developing early childhood cognitive development in the development of gadget technology and current social media.

Early childhood is a golden age where brain cell growth as an area of cognitive potential begins to develop rapidly when properly stimulated will have a positive impact on future development. Therefore stimulation of the YouTube video can be used as a reference for parents at home to develop children's intelligence to be more efficient and practical with this stimulation note carried out with appropriate guidance and guidance by parents.

Suggestion

For the Society

Due to the development of technology that facilitates access to all kinds of needs, this research is expected to provide an overview for the community about the positive scientific impact of psychology in developing early childhood cognitive use YouTube media with proper guidance and guidance by parents.

For Further Research

It is hoped that there will be further research that uses a qualitative and quantitative approach simultaneously to obtain a more comprehensive picture of early childhood cognitive development.

References

1. Berk , Laura E *Development Though The Lifespan* (edisi kelima). Terj. Darmanto, Yogyakarta: Pustaka Pelajar, 2012).
2. Brad & Debra Scheep, *How to Make Money With You Tube.* New York: McGraw-Hill Education (2009).
3. Departemen Kesehatan Republik Indonesia *Pedoman Deteksi Dini Tumbuh Kembang Balita*, Departemen Kesehatan Republik Indonesia (2006).
4. Desmita *Psikologi Perkembangan*, Bandung :Remaja Rosdyakarya Offset (2013).
5. Fadillah Muhammad *Desain Pembelajaran PAUD*, Tinjauan Teoritik dan Praktik Yogyakarta: Ar-Ruzz media (2012).
6. Fort, mathilde *Audio Visual Vowel Monitoring and the Word Superiority* Effect in Chidren International Journal of Behafioral Development. (2012).

7. Hanisah. *Meningkatkan Kecerdasan Intrapersonal Anak Melalui Kegiatan Bercerita Berbantuan Media Film /VCD dikelompok B5 RA Ummat An Wahidah di Kota Curup.* Skripsi kependidikan Bagi Guru, Universitas Bengkulu. ,(2014)

8. Jahja, Yudrik *Psikologi Perkembangan*, Jakarta: Kencana (2011).

9. Kurniawati, Ita. *Pengaruh Media Audio Visual pencampuran Warna terhadap Kemampuan Kognitif pada Anak Kelompok A TK My Children Kee. Candi Kabupaten Sidoarjo.* (2013

10. Syaodih Mubiar Agustin, Ernawulan *Bimbingan Konseling Untuk Anak Usia Dini,* Jakarta: UT (2011).

11. https://www.nesabamedia.com/pengertian-youtube/ Pengertian Youtube Beserta Manfaat dan Fitur-fitur Youtube yang Perlu Anda Ketahui

Development of Natural Science Learning Media in Primary School Using Flash Applications to Increase Student's Achievement

Hindayati Mustafidah[1,*], *Muhammad Gilang Audi Imani*[1], *Sriyanto*[2], *and Suwarsito*[2]

[1]Faculty of Engineering – Universitas Muhammadiyah Purwokerto, Jl. Raya Dukuhwaluh Purwokerto, Central Java, Indonesia 53182
[2] Faculty of Education – Universitas Muhammadiyah Purwokerto, Jl. Raya Dukuhwaluh Purwokerto, Central Java, Indonesia 53182

Abstract. The negative impact of the development of information technology in the form of smartphones triggers students lazy to learn. But the positive impact can increase student activity and learning achievement because students can play while learning. This was experienced by students of Qaryah Thayyibah Elementary School in Purwokerto, Indonesia. In the process of teaching and learning at the elementary school is still using books so that students' interest in learning is lacking, especially science subjects. But on the other hand, students really like playing with their smartphones. This is the reason for doing research on the development of Android-based learning media using the Flash application. The method used in conducting this research is the Multimedia Development Life Cycle (MDLC). The development of this multimedia method is carried out based on six stages, namely concept, design, collecting material, assembly, testing, and distribution. Based on the results of testing on students, using flash applications in science subjects can provide solutions to optimize student learning processes. This is evidenced by the increase in student scores by 7.275%, namely before using the application has an average value of 7.56 ± 0.726 and after using the learning media application increased to 8.11 ± 0.821.

1 Introduction

Widespread use and dependence of information technology in the wider community is undeniably giving rise to concerns among various circles, including educators and parents. Many teachers and parents worry that the widespread use of communication and information technology can have an adverse impact on children. Some things that seem to be very much a concern for parents are the possibility of children easily accessing various pornographic or porno actions, as well as the effects of addiction on social media and games, especially online games. This impact will certainly interfere with the concentration of children's learning, and later make children more happy to be alone so that their social sensitivity develops is not optimal.

Learning in schools today still tends to be monotonous, where learning is not yet student-centered. Although the government has launched scientific learning with the enactment of the 2013 Curriculum, in reality the learning applied in several schools is still relatively monotonous, with teacher-centeredness. This learning model does not prioritize action on students but more on the lecture process conducted by the teacher while students listen passively. As an example of a case in Qaryah Thayyibah Purwokerto Elementary School (SD QITA), information was obtained that many students felt easily bored with the amount of material, as well as difficult terms that needed to be memorized in science lessons. Teachers feel they must always find new strategies so that their students are not bored, and more motivated to learn. On the other hand, parents and teachers are also worried about their children's interest in smartphones. Based on interviews with several parents, it was obtained data that children tend to be difficult to be asked to study at home. They are much more enthusiastic about picking up gadgets, especially smartphones, rather than to reading books or notebooks.

Based on the reasons that have been conveyed, it takes an alternative problem solving that can facilitate children's needs for communication and information technology, as well as being a means of active and interactive learning activities that are not monotonous. Therefore, a learning media based on communication and information technology is built, which can be used as a learning tool at home, so that children do not monotonically learn only by memorizing through textbooks. In this media contains materials and exercises about science subjects in class III elementary school chapter 1 through chapter 5.

Media is an intermediary or messenger from the sender to the recipient of the message. Media can be human, material, or events that build conditions that make students able to acquire knowledge, skills, or attitudes [1]. Learning media is a means to establish communication interactions that are educational between teachers and students [2] as well as channeling messages

* Corresponding author: fida.mustafidah@ump.ac.id

or content, stimulating students' thoughts, feelings, attention and abilities, so as to encourage teaching and learning [3-4]. The learning media in question are books, tape recorders, cassettes, video cameras, video recorders, films, slides (pictures), photos, pictures, graphics, television and computers. This is a form of implementation of the contents of Law RI No.20 of 2003 which states that learning is the process of interaction of students with educators and learning resources in a learning environment. Information technology-based learning media can be applied with tutorial, simulation, and games models, including the use of the internet in it as a medium of knowledge transfer from one device to another or transfer of information between media [5] and [6].

Some advantages of ICT integration in the learning process are suggested by [7], [8], [9]. This is evidenced by several results of research conducted by [10] who developed Adobe Flash CS5-based science learning media and showed that there was a significant increase in the quality of learning seen from the responses of students and teachers' interests. Another study of learning media development was conducted by [11] which showed an increase in learning motivation for students of Grade 5 of the Dagen 1 Public Elementary School in Jaten. Mobile multimedia had been developed by [12] to present of descriptive studies showed an increase in the ability to understand colors and letters in class 1 elementary school students, and [13] aimed at testing the impact of use multimedia program with Adobe Flash, achieving results of increasing student academic achievement.

Long before ICTs developed as they are today, ICT-based learning media can also improve students' understanding in reading the Qur'an [14]. In addition, the improvement of understanding and achievement of junior high school students and university students can also be enhanced by ICT-based learning media [15], [16], [17], [18]. Other research is to implement multimedia applications with animated cartoons on science learning in elementary schools, which results in an increase in student interest [19].

2 Method

2.1. Data Collection

This application in the form of learning media was built using AdobeFlash CS6 software with Actionscrip 3.0 programming language for grade III elementary school science materials. The research data was collected from interviews with teachers related to the curriculum, observation to find out the learning activities that took place in Purwokerto QITA Elementary School and how the teacher delivered the material and the things students did during the learning process, and the third grade elementary science material documentation.

2.2 System Engineering

The application was designed using the Multimedia Development Life Cycle (MDLC) model as shown in Fig. 1.

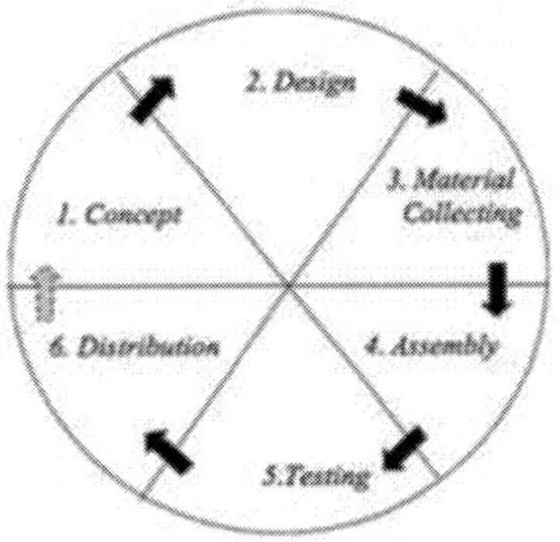

Fig. 1. SDLC Model for Application Development [20].

Concept. The concept stage is the stage to determine the goals and who will use the application. At this stage it is designed as to what this application will be made.

Design. The design phase is the stage of making specifications regarding the program architecture, appearance and material requirements for the program. The hardware requirements needed for the implementation of this application are a set of computers and an Android Mobile unit. This learning media is built based on applications with the Android operating system that is open source and runs on mobile devices that are commonly used by the public with various advantages [21], [22], [23]. Software requirements needed for the implementation of this application are Adobe Flash CS6, Adobe Photoshop CS6, Flash Player, and Adobe AIR. Application design is used by Unified Modeling Language (UML) with use case diagrams and activity diagrams. As the main media development software, Adobe Photoshop as an image editor software is devoted to photo/image editing and effect making [24] and Macromedia Flash to produce interactive, interesting and dynamic presentations and movie games and various other advantages [12], [25], [26]. Action script as an Adobe Flash programming language is used to create animations or interactions [27]. Unifield Modeling Language (UML) is used for the purposes of visualizing, designing and documenting the system [28]. Use case diagrams and activity diagrams are used to find out what functions are in the system and who has the right to use these functions, as well as describing the various flow of activities in the system [29]. Activity diagrams and use case diagrams are presented in Fig. 2, 3, 4 and 5.

Material Collecting is a process for collecting data in the form of material presented in an application, multimedia files such as audio and images needed in multimedia presentation.

Assembly. This stage is the conversion phase of the design into the form of program code that can be understood by the machine. The encoding is done using Actionscript 3.0.

Testing. This phase includes the overall testing of applications that have been built using the Black Box Testing Method [30].

Distribution. At this stage, the application is processed into an *.apk file. After becoming an *.apk file, this application is ready to be published for users.

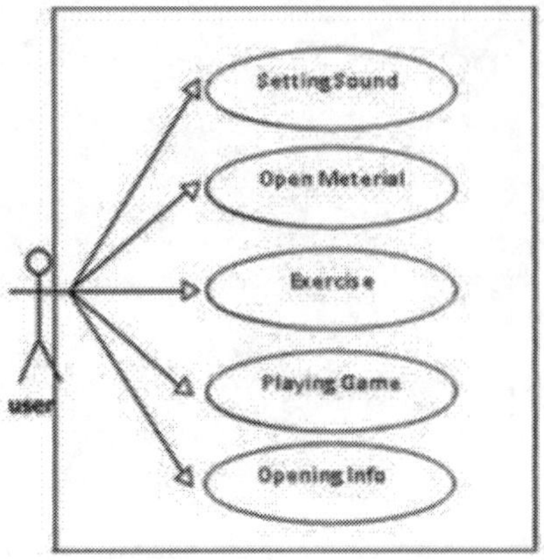

Fig. 2. SDLC Model for Application Development

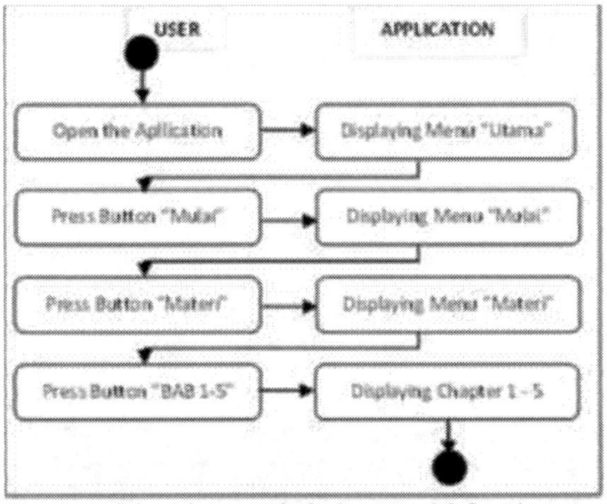

Fig. 3. Activity Diagram Displaying Material for Elementary School Science in the Third Grade

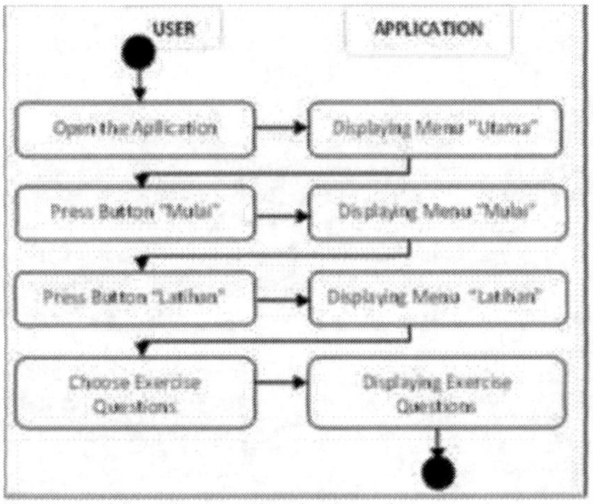

Fig. 4. Activity Diagram Showing Exercise

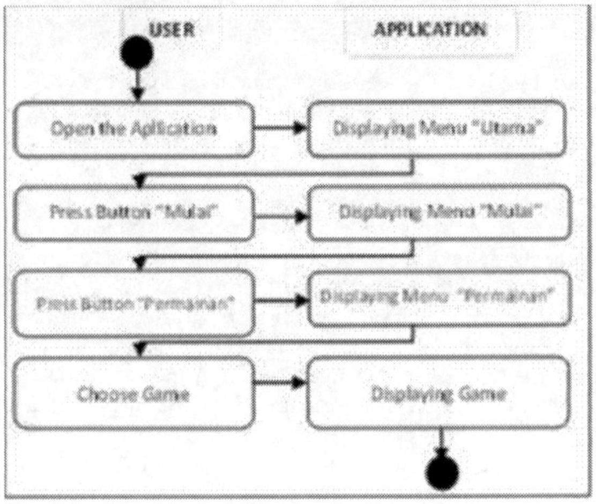

Fig. 5. Activity Diagram Showing the Game

2.3 Measurement of Student Learning Achievement

Measurement of student achievement scores is done before and after using the application. Measurements were carried out by testing applications that had been developed for third grade students at QITA Elementary School as research samples.

3 RESULTS AND DISCUSSION

3.1 Learning Media Application

The learning media application produced from this study is a .apk file with version 1.0 that is ready to run on smartphone devices based on the Android operating system. This application contains third grade elementary school science materials with interesting animations and pictures to improve student learning interest, and make students easier to understand the material presented. The material presented is chapter 1 to chapter 5 or the same as the implementation of learning in 1 semester. In this learning media there is also a practice question that can be used as an ability test tool for students. The problem consists of 10 items with 3 minutes working time. After students work on the questions, the application will immediately display the scores obtained by students. This application is also equipped with discussion of questions and answer keys.

The learning media application produced consists of several menus, namely the "Utama", "Mulai", "Materi", "Soal", and "Permainan" menus. Menu "Utama" is the main menu that first appears when the application is run. There are 3 buttons on the main menu, namely Enter ("Masuk"), Sound, Info (Fig. 6). The Enter button serves to display the 4 core sub menus of this application namely Material, Exercise, Games, and Exit. Sound button functions to activate and deactivate music. The info button contains the function of the third grade science teaching learning media for elementary school in 1 semester.

Fig. 6. Main Menu of the Third Class Natural Science Learning Application

The **Start** menu has 4 menus where each menu has its own function (Fig. 7). Menu Material contains 5 CHAPTER menus on the subject matter of grade III science subjects. The Problem menu contains a menu of practice questions for each chapter. Menu Games contain various games according to the material presented.

Fig. 7. Start Menu Interface

The **"MATERI"** menu is included in the main menu, in which there are 5 BAB menus, and includes the Home menu to return to the Start menu. The chapter menu contains class III science subjects in accordance with the existing chapter (Fig. 8).

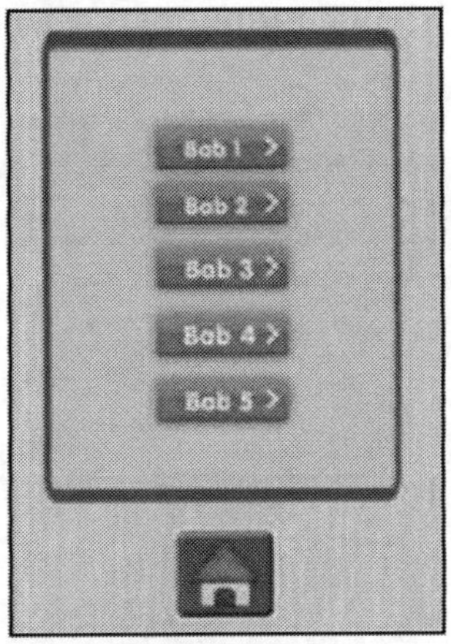

Fig. 8. Menu "MATERI" Interface

Fig. 8 is a view that appears on the Material menu. If the user presses CHAPTER 1 button, it will display the material about CHAPTER 1 (Fig. 9), the CHAPTER 2 button will display CHAPTER 2 material (Fig. 10), and so on until CHAPTER 5.

Fig. 9. CHAPTER 1 Interface on the MATERI Menu

Fig. 10. CHAPTER 2 Interface on the MATERI Menu

The Question menu is included in the main menu, in which there is a sub menu of practice questions from CHAPTER 1- 5. The following is a menu display of the questions (Fig. 11). If the user presses one of the sub-menu buttons on the question menu, a new display will appear containing an explanation of how to do the practice question (Fig. 12).

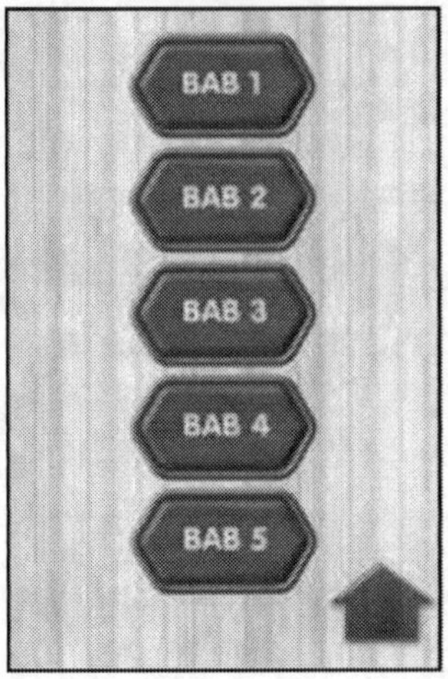

Fig. 11. Interface Question Menu

Fig. 12. Display of CHAPTER 1 Exercise

If user presses the work button, the question will be displayed. The time to do the questions is given for 3 minutes (180 seconds) as in Fig. 13.

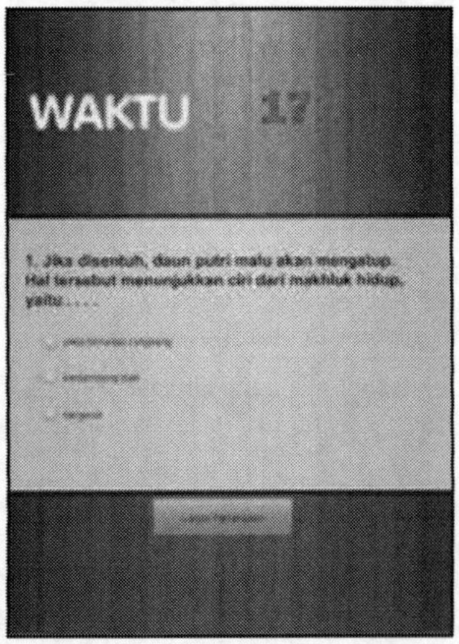

Fig. 13. Display of Exercise Questions

If the user runs out of time when working then the application will automatically display the score of the results of the exercise that has been done (Fig. 14).

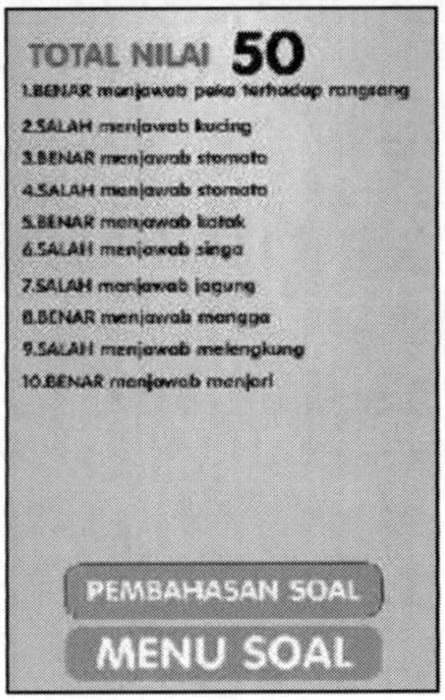

Fig. 14. Score Display

In the score display there is a discussion menu to discuss the questions contained in the practice questions according to the chapter (Fig. 15).

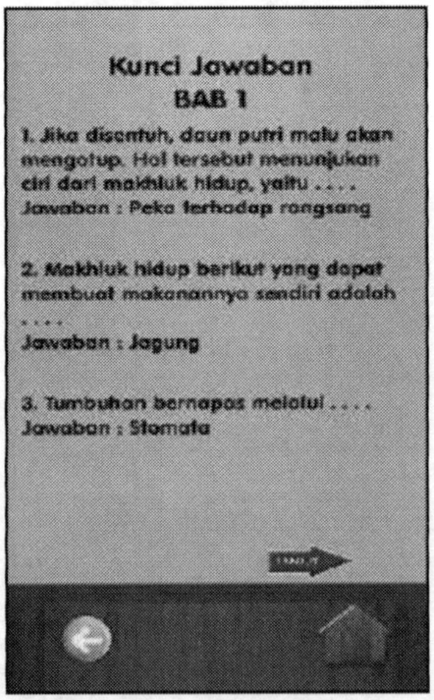

Fig. 15. Discussion of Practice Questions

Game menu is created with the aim of attracting user interest to learn. Besides users can learn, users can play with games that are appropriate for their age also. There are 5 game sub menus in this game menu (Fig. 16).

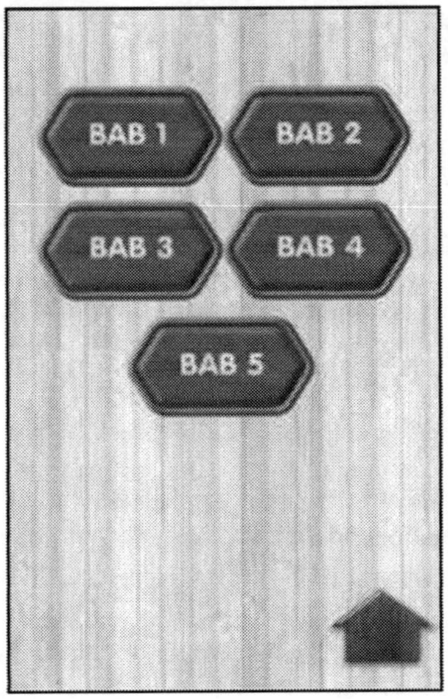

Fig. 16. Game Menu Display

Game 1 is taken from chapter 1 material about living things. The rules of playing game 1, the user must look for plant-eating animals (Fig. 17).

Fig. 17. Game 1 Display

If the user is wrong in choosing the image of the animal then the application will automatically display as in Fig. 18. If the user is correct in choosing the image of the animal then the application will automatically display as in Fig. 19.

Fig. 18. Wrong Display in Game 1

Fig. 19. Right Display in Game 1

Game 2 is taken from CHAPTER 2 material that is about changes in living things. In the game 2 users must move animal images according to the method of breeding. Furthermore, game 3 was taken from CHAPTER 3, which is about the environment. In the game 3 users have to throw garbage in its place by moving the garbage image to the trash can. Meanwhile, game 4 was taken from the CHAPTER 4 material about the object and its nature. In game 4 the user must choose the object that is the writing instrument. The last game, game 5, was taken from CHAPTER 5 about changes in the nature of objects. In this game 5 the user must move the image according to the way it changes its nature. In each game, if the user succeeds in playing it, information will be displayed "SUCCESSFUL" ("BERHASIL") and vice versa will be displayed "FALSE" ("SALAH") if the user incorrectly plays it.

3.2 System Testing

The system that has been built is tested using the blackbox method to the functions that are in the application that is by running each menu and buttons to see if there are errors or not. Based on the test results on each menu and button, it is stated that there is no error in the application.

3.3 Measurement of Student Learning Achievement

Student achievement after using this learning media is presented in Table 1. The number of students who were sampled in this study was 9 students.

Table 1. Results of student learning achievement.

No.	Score Before	Score After
1	6	6
2	7	8
3	7	8
4	8	8.5
5	8	8.5
6	8	8.5
7	8	8.5
8	8	8.5
9	8	8.5

Based on the data in Table 1, a correlation analysis was carried out on the two research variables, namely the students' scores before using the learning media and after using the learning media (Table 2) and the analysis using the t-test to determine the average differences of the two research variables.

Table 2. Font styles for a reference to a journal article.

		N	Correlation	Sig.
Pair 1	Pre & Post	9	.932	.000

Correlation test results in Table 2 for 2 paired samples obtained a significance of 0.00 (smaller than $\alpha = 0.05$). This shows that the two research variables namely the value of students before and after using learning media have a strong correlation of 0.932. In addition, the results of the analysis using the t-test showed that the two study variables had a significant average difference at the level of $\alpha = 5\%$. Bu using SPSS software shows that the average score of students after using learning media is higher than before using learning media. Overall the achievement of students' scores in the science subject descriptively before using the application has an average value of 7.56 ± 0.726 and after using the learning media application rose to 8.11 ± 0.821.

4 CONCLUSION

The conclusion of this study is to use Android-based learning media applications on subjects of Natural Sciences for elementary school class III can provide solutions to optimize student learning processes. This is evidenced by the increase in value for students after using the application which is an increase of 7.275%.

References

[1] Hamruni, *Strategi Pembelajaran*. Yogyakarta: Insan Madani, 2013.

[2] A. Arsyad, "Media pembelajaran." Jakarta: PT Raja Grafindo Persada, 2011.

[3] I. Ibrahim and S. Syaodih, *Perencanaan Pembelajaran*. Jakarta: Rineka Cipta, 2013.

[4] Moedjiono, "Tantangan dan Peluang Teknologi Informasi dan Komunikasi dalam Peningkatan Kesejahteraan Masyarakat Indonesia," *J. Atmaluhur*, vol. 1, no. 2, pp. 2–8, 2014.

[5] Darmawan, *Pendidikan Teknologi Informasi dan Komunikasi*. Bandung: Rosda Karya, 2013.

[6] Depdiknas, *Naskah Akademik Kajian Kebijakan Kurikulum Mata Pelajaran TIK*. Jakarta: Depdiknas, 2013.

[7] Sutarman, *Pengantar Teknologi Informasi*. Jakarta: Bumi Aksara, 2013.

[8] Supriyanto, *Pengantar Teknologi Informasi*. Jakarta: Salemba Infotek, 2014.

[9] UNESCO, "ICT Transforming Education: A Regional Guide," 2015. [Online]. Available: http://www.unesco.org/ new/ en/ communication-and-information/ resources/ publications- and-communication-materials/publications/full-list/ict-transforming-education-a-regional-guide/. [Accessed: 04-Jun-2017].

[10] Prasetyaningsih, "Pengembangan Media Pembelajaran IPA Berbasis Adobe Flash CS5 untuk Siswa Kelas V Sekolah Dasar," Universitas PGRI Yogyakarta, 2015.

[11] I. Iswahyudi and U. Urbani, "Pembuatan Media Pembelajaran Ilmu Pengetahuan Alam Kelas 5 Sekolah Dasar Negeri Dagen 1 Jateng," in *Prosiding Seminar Riset Unggulan Nasional Informatika dan Komputer FTI UNSA 2013, ISSN: 2302-1136. Volume 2, No. 1, Maret 2013*, 2013.

[12] Sutopo, "Mobile Multimedia Development : Flash Mobile Game with MySQL Database," *Int. J. Comput. Theory Eng.*, vol. 5, no. 1, pp. 47–54, 2013.

[13] I. Shah and M. Khan, "Impact of Multimedia-aided Teaching on Students' Academic Achievement and Attitude at Elementary," *US-China Educ. Rev. A*, vol. 5, no. 5, pp. 349–360, 2015.

[14] H. Mustafidah and Nurhidayah, "Rancangbangun Multimedia Pembelajaran Ilmu Tajwid Guna

Peningkatan Pemahaman Cara Membaca Al-Qur'an," *JUITA (Jurnal Inform.*, vol. 1, no. 2, pp. 31–37, 2010.

[15] L. A. Purwanto, H. Mustafidah, and D. K. Hakim, "Pengembangan Media Pembelajaran Matematika Geometri Bangun Ruang Sisi Lengkung Berbasis Multimedia Guna Meningkatkan Minat dan Prestasi Siswa SMPN 1 Patikraja," in *Prosiding Seminar Nasional dan Call for Paper "Inovasi Teknologi Ramah Lingkungan dalam Perspektif Pemanasan Global" , 31 Maret 2012*, 2012.

[16] H. Mustafidah and N. Kurniasih, "Pengembangan Media Pembelajaran Berbasis Komputer Guna Meningkatkan Pemahaman Mahasiswa pada Mata Kuliah Metode Numerik," *BIOMATH*, vol. X, no. 1, pp. 1–11, 2009.

[17] H. Mustafidah and D. Ariyanto, "Pengembangan Media Pembelajaran Digital Interaktif Kalkulus-II dalam Peningkatan Prestasi Belajar Mahasiswa," *Techno*, vol. 11, no. 2, pp. 84–93, 2010.

[18] E. Setyaningsih and H. Mustafidah, "Pengembangan Media Pembelajaran Berbasis Komputer pada Pokok Bahasan Himpunan Guna Meningkatkan Pemahaman Mahasiswa," *JUITA (Jurnal Inform.*, vol. 1, no. 2, pp. 45–51, 2010.

[19] Dalacosta, "Multimedia application with animated cartoons for teaching science in elementary education," *J. Comput. Educ. Arch.*, vol. 52, no. 4, pp. 741–748, 2009.

[20] I. Binanto, *Multimedia Digital – Dasar Teori dan Pengembangannya*. Yogyakarta: ANDI, 2014.

[21] Safaat, *Pemrograman Aplikasi Mobile Smartphone dan Tables PC Berbasis Android*. Bandung: Informatika, 2014.

[22] Winarto, *Membuat Aplikasi Android untuk Pemula*. Jakarta: Kompas Gramedia, 2013.

[23] Utami, *Kupas Tuntas Android dari Nol Sampai Bisa*. Jakarta: Gudang Ilmu, 2014.

[24] Permana, *Penuntun Praktis Adobe Photoshop 7.0*. Jakarta: Elex Media Komputindo, 2013.

[25] Madcoms, *Mahir dalam 7 Hari Macromedia Flash Pro 8*. Jakarta: Gramedia, 2013.

[26] Anggra, *Pembuatan Game berbasis Flash*. Yogyakarta: Gava Media, 2013.

[27] Ariesto, *Animasi dengan Macromedia Flash + Action Script*. Jakarta: Salemba Empat, 2013.

[28] G. Booch, J. Rumbaugh, and I. Jacobson, *The Unified Modeling Language User Guide*, 2nd ed. Canada: Addison-Wesley Professional, 2005.

[29] M. F. Rentor, "Rancang Bangun Perangkat Lunak Pengenalan Motif Batik Berbasis Augmented Reality." UAJY, 2013.

[30] M. Shalahuddin and S. Rosa, *Modul Pembelajaran Rekayasa Perangkat Lunak*. Bandung: Modula, 2013.

Analysis of Elementary School Teachers' Work Discipline at UPTD Education in Banyumanik, Semarang City

Muhamad Afandi [1,*], *Zulela* MS[2], and *Amos* Neolaka[3]

[1]Elementary Teacher Education, Sultan Agung Islamic University, Indonesia
[2]Department of Elementary Education. State University of Jakarta, Indonesia
[3]Department of Elementary Education. State University of Jakarta, Indonesia

Abstract. This study is aimed to describe the elementary school teachers' work discipline at the UPTD Education in Banyumanik, Semarang City. The study involved 162 elementary school teachers. The instrument used in this study was a questionnaire consisting of 30 statement items, and 5 indicators of work discipline for elementary school teachers. The findings showed that each indicator of discipline of time was very good (90.8), discipline of work was good (90.1), discipline in work atmosphere was very good (91.4), discipline in serving community was good (88,9), discipline of attitude and behavior was sufficient (75). Overall, the work discipline of elementary school teachers was good (87). These findings indicated that the elementary school teachers at the UPTD education in Banyumanik, Semarang City worked in well-discipline.

Keywords: *work discipline, teacher and elementary school*

1 Introduction

Education, as stated in Act Number 20 of 2003 concerning National Education System, is a process carried out consciously and planned to actualize fun learning atmosphere and learning processes so that students become very active and develop their potentials in order to increase their knowledge, insight and experience to determine their life goals, by which they can eventually gain broader insight for a better future.

The purpose of national education as explained in Article 3 is to develop students' potentials in order to become faithful and fearful humanbeings to God Almighty, noble, healthy, knowledgeable, capable, creative, independent, disciplined, responsible and democratic citizens. (Act Number 20 of 2003, 2012). Education is a process in which practice involves various aspects to support students' success and to develop their existing potentials, either cognitive, affective or psychomotor aspects. Education is also a basic need in human life because humanbeing education will always count on knowledge, attitudes, and habits which are in accordance with existing norms (Afandi & Yustiana, 2018).

Education of discipline character is an important thing to consider in order to foster a person's character. Armed with the value of discipline character will encourage the growth of other good character values, such as responsibility, honesty, cooperation, and so on (Wuryandani, Maftuh, & Budimansyah, 2014). Undisciplinary behavior is also often found in school environments, including elementary schools. Some examples of such undisciplined behavior are including; late coming to school, wearing incomplete uniform in accordance with what's stated in the school rules, sitting or walking comfortably on grass with clear written notification "*prohibited to steping on the grass*", littering, scribbling on the walls of schools, skipping school, submitting tasks late, not putting uniforms on according to the rules, and so on.

Discipline stated in (Government Regulation, 2010) concerning the Discipline of Civil Servants is explained that discipline is the ability of Civil Servants to comply with obligations and avoid prohibitions specified in the legislation and/or official regulations with respect to giving penalty to those who violate and disobeyed. In addition, various rules established by a school or educational institution have a very important role in creating discipline so that teachers can comply with and implement the rules. The rules or norms are usually followed by sanctions given when they are found violating. The sanctions can be in the form of both oral and written reprimands, suspension, degrading position,

* Corresponding author: mafandi@unissula.ac.id

and even job dismissal. It depends on the amount of violations committed by a teacher.

This is in line with the explanation (Wuryandani et al., 2014) that educator's moral and character have a major role in students' moral development through a hidden curriculum manifested in interpersonal environment of schools and classrooms. In classroom, teachers need to do various things to support the success of the discipline character education program, among which are having a very close and warm relationship with students, turning classroom into a laboratory discipline for students, controlling the students' behavior, and provide time to address the issue of behavior which is not in accordance with the rules that should be.

It is intended that teachers work in discipline and become responsible for their work. If thier work discipline is very high, it is expected that they can complete assignments quickly and precisely so that job satisfaction arises (Mulyasa, 2013).

Thus, it is clear that the teacher's work discipline is the main factor which determines the success of learning quality in elementary schools. Thus in this article describes discipline of elementary school teachers'are adjusted to schedule, therefore, this study is aimed at describing the elementary school at the UPTD education, Banyumanik, Semarang City.

2 Research Method

The research method used was quantitative descriptive. The research site was carried out in all state elementary schools at UPTD Education Bayumanik, Semarang City, Central Java, as many as 31 schools. Population is a generalization area consisting of objects with certain quantity and characteristics determined by researchers to be studied and then drawn to conclusions (Sugiyono, 2016) .

The population in this study were State Elementary School teachers at UPTD Education Banyumanik, Semarang City, with a total of 7 Teacher Working Groups, and the overall class teachers were 272 community. In this study, the sampling technique was done by using *simple random sampling of area* with sampling respondent determination in lottery. The samples gained in this study were 162 teachers. The sampling technique was conducted by random method of each UPTD Education Group in Banyumanik, Semarang City. The determination of the teachers was drawn based on the Teacher Working Group, then the teachers in each school were randomly sampled with the reason that each school and teacher of each school had the same opportunity as a sample.

The data collection of this study was conducted using questionnaire. Questionnaire is a technique or method of collecting data indirectly (the researcher did not directly ask the respondents). The questionnaire instrument contained a number of questions or statements that must be answered or responded by the respondents (Sumadinata, 2013)

To capture information or data from the respondents, the research instruments are prepared. The questionnaire instrumets were made based on conceptuality, including conceptual definition, operational definition, and research instrument guideliness, instrument calibration, Validity and Realiability Testing. The number of statements has four alternative answers. The measurement scales of the questionnaire instruments were made based on Likert scale with four alternative answers, namely: (1) Always with a score of 4 , (2) Often with a score of 3 , (3) Sometimes with a score of 2 , (4) Never with a score of 1.

The research data were collected, analyzed descriptively with the criteria in accordance with the regulation of minister of Utilization of State Apparatus and Bureaucratic Reform 2009 article 15 as follows; a. values of 91 to 100 are called very good; b. values of 76 to 90 are called good; c. values of 61 to 75 are sufficient; d. values of 51 to 60 are called medium; and e. values up to 50 are called less.

3 Findings And Discussion

3.1 Findings

The findings of this study focus on those related to the work discipline of elementary school teachers, which was composed of discipline of time, discipline of work, discipline in working atmosphere, discipline in serving community, discipline of attitude and behavior.

Based on the data analysis, it was found that the average score was 87 for work discipline with '*good*' criteria. In addition, based on the number of teachers participating in this study, there was discipline criteria of teacher work from 162 teachers, 60 teachers were identified (37.04%) with '*very good*' work discipline criteria, there were 85 teachers (52.47%) on the criteria of '*good*', there were 16 teachers (9.88%) on the criteria of '*sufficient*', and there was 1 teacher (0.62%) on the criteria of '*medium*'.

Meanwhile, the achievement of the indicators of elementary school teachers' work discipline, which was composed of time discipline, work discipline, working atmosphere discipline, discipline in serving community, discipline in attitude and behavior at the UPTD education Banyumanik are presented in Table 1

Table 1. Data of Work Discipline Result of Elementary School Teachers.

No	Indicators	Score	Criteria
1	Discipline in time	90.8	Very Good
2	Discipline in work	90.1	Good
3	Discipline inwork atmosphere	91.4	Very Good
4	Discipline in serving community	88.9	Good

5	Discipline in attitude and behavior	75	Sufficient
Average		**87**	**Good**

The data showed that the score of elementary school teachers' work discipline on each indicator as follows; the discipline in time was 90.8, the discipline in work was 90.1, the discipline in work atmosphere was 91.4, the discipline in serving the community was 88.9, the discipline in attitude and behavior was 75. The average score of the five indicators was 87 and classified as '*good*'.

The indicator of discipline in time of the elementary school teachers was classified as "*very good*". This shows that the teacher had already had discipline in time, both obeying task time, using time well, and completing the task on time.

The Indicator of discipline in teachers' work was classified as '*good*', showing that teachers owned discipline in work based on three item statements, namely complying with work rules, preparing teaching equipments, and performing basic tasks.

The implementation of discipline in teaching atmosphere was at the criteria of '*good*' based on sub- indicator, namely utilization of work environment, good relationships and maintaining rights and obligations so as to balance.

The implementation of discipline in serving community was in '*good*' criteria. The highest criterion was in the statement item of serving students with very good criteria. Whereas, in the criteria, both seen from discipline in serving community were the teacher's discipline in serving students, parents and the surrounding community.

The indicator of discipline of elementary school teachers' attitude and behavior was in the criteria of '*good*'. In this case, for the statement concerning behavior, it needs to be improved because it is in sufficient criteria, while the highest criteria are in the statement item, paying attention to attitudes and self-esteem, which were with good criteria.

3.2 Discussion

The findings indicate that the work discipline of Banyumanik Elementary School Teachers in Semarang City was at the criteria of '*good*' as proven by the results of the instrument on teacher work discipline, which consists of five indicators, namely discipline of time, discipline of work, discipline of work atmosphere, discipline in serving community, discipline of attitudes and behavior.

First, in the discipline of time, teachers were asked dealing with time, either to obey tasks, to manage time well and to complete the tasks on time, the findings showed that the elementary school teachers' discipline was very good. As confirmed by (Danim, 2015) that self-discipline *(self-discipline)* as the ability to position yourself to take action regardless of the emotional atmosphere. In other words, self-discipline is a self-control and a self-consistency. For a teacher, teacher discipline is the ability of the teacher to position himself to take certain actions in accordance with substance, procedure, time limit, and criteria for them goals to achieve.

Second, the discipline of teachers' work, whether obeying work rules, preparing teaching, equipments, and carrying out the main tasks, the findings of the study indicate that the elementary school teachers had the discipline of work with the criteria of '*good*'. (Aqib, 2012) asserts that discipline is an action displaying orderly behavior and complying with various rules and regulations. In line with Aqib, stating that work discipline is an attitude, behavior, and action that is in accordance with rules both written and unwritten, and if violating, there will be sanctions for the violations. (Susanty & Baskoro, 2012) In line with (Rahman, 2014) state that implementing discipline is an important activity which needs to be done to improve the discipline of teachers at school, because the core of the coaching discipline is discipline itself firmly especially in providing sanctions to those who violate the discipline. The provision of sanctions is intended to raise awareness so as not to violate work discipline, such as a delay between when a goal is formulated and when that goal is achieved.

Third, the discipline of the teachers' atmosphere by utilizing the work environment, establishing good relationships and maintaining a balance between rights and obligations, the findings of the study showed that the elementary school teachers were in the criteria of '*good*'. (Stanley, 2014) emphasizes that discipline and academic performance is the key to success in the field of education and both are strategies used to instill positive behavior and character of students, self-control and regulatory compliance at school. The same thing was conveyed by (Arianto, 2013) that the indicators of the work culture of the teaching staff are as follows: (1) the physical environmental conditions of work, including: awarding, providing welfare, fulfilling infrastructure and facilities. (2) work environment conditions, including: support in carrying out tasks, being able to design work, supervision and work discipline, communication and interaction with peers, parents of students, principals and community environment, principal's leadership functions, establishing individual policies, school programs in accordance with the nature and objectives, setting compensation policies and school management.

Fourth, the implementation of discipline in serving community with sub-indicators of serving students, parents and the surrounding communities, the findings showed that the elementary school teachers had discipline in serving the community with 'good' criteria. (Niesche, 2010) reveals that community or environment discipline is a period of social control where power is no longer used to punish individuals who violate, but to improve their potential. To achieve this, there needs to be a mechanism that can function corrective as an evaluation of various elements of society.

Fifth, the discipline of attitudes and behavior with sub-indicators, such as paying attention to attitudes, behavior and self-esteem, the findings of the study showed that the elementary school teachers had the discipline of attitudes and behavior with '*good*' criteria. Affirmed by (Walters & Frei, 2007), dicipline is related to how someone behaves, namely management and self-control. Therefore, classroom management is the teachers' responsibility. In line with (Susanty & Baskoro, 2012), work discipline is an attitude, behavior and deed based on rules both written and unwritten, and if there is a violation, there will be sanctions for the violation.

The teachers'work discipline consisted of these five indicators, namely discpline of time, discipline of work, discipline of work atmosphere, discipline in serving community, discipline of attitudes and behavior, must be owned by teachers in order to guarantee the quality of the implementation of learning process in elementary school.

In this study, work discipline refers to attitude of obedience, loyalty and awareness of elementary school teachers toward applicable regulations in the form of behavior and actions in an organization to achieve a certain goal. The indicators to measure work discipline, such as discipline of time, discipline of work, discipine in work atmosphere, discipline in serving community, and discipline of attitudes and behavior.

As confirmed in the opinion of (Shih, Wu, Lai, & Liao, 2015) that lately, positive discipline attitude is the main thing in school and every educator must have this attitude so that it can improve the quality of learning and have a direct impact on the students' attitudes and discipline. Similar opinions expressed by (Rahimi & Karkami, 2015), stating that teacher discipline strategies can have a positive impact on the students' learning and protect them from cognitive and emotional threats. In this case, it can be hypothesized that when teachers are disciplined, involviong students in decision-making and recognizing each student's character, students will be more responsible in the classroom.

Based on this statement, it can be said that the role of discipline is absolutely necessary in the world of education. Lack of teachers' discipline can decrease the quality of learning in the classroom as well as trigger negative actions of students, such as disobedient to school rules, late, violence, drug abuse and so on.

Most of the discipline behavior in everyday classroom activities is not clearly written in the learning implementation plan made by the teacher. Most are in the form of hidden curricula which are manifested in teachers' daily behavior. The teachers' discipline in entering classroom, wearing uniforms, managing the class is all considered by students..

4 Conclusion

The description of the implementation of work discipline of the elementary school teachers at UPTD education in Banyumanik, Semarang city is in '*good*' criteria. This is indicated with an average score of 87. Furthermore, the acquisition of each indicator as follows: discipline of time is very good (90,8), discipline of work is good (90.1), discipline in work atmosphere is very good (91.4), discipline in serving community is good (88.9), discipline of attitude and behavior is enough (75).

5 Acknowledgement

The researcher delivers his gratitudes to the Directorate of Research and Community Service, Directorate General of Research and Development, Ministry of Research, Technology and Higher Education of the Republic of Indonesia who have provided Doctoral dissertation grant to complete research and doctoral program studies. This article is part of dissertation research to complete the Doctor in Elementary Education at Postgraduate Program of University of Jakarta.

References

1. Aqib, Z. (2012) Pendidikan karakter di Sekolah. Bandung: Yama Widya
2. Afandi, M., & Yustiana, S. (2018). The Performance of Primary School Teachers In the Unit of Education Technical Implementation, *1*(2), 81–91. Retrieved from https://ejournal.unri.ac.id/index.php/JTLEE/article/view/5878
3. Arianto, D. A. N. (2013). Pengaruh Kedisiplinan, Lingkungan Kerja Dan Budaya Kerja Terhadap Kinerja Tenaga Pengajar. *Jurnal Economia*, *9*(2), 191–200.
4. Mulyasa. (2013). *Pengembangan dan Implementasi Kurikulum 2013*. Bandung: Rosda Karya.
5. Niesche, R. (2010). Discipline through documentation: A form of governmentality for school principals. *International Journal of Leadership in Education*, *13*(3), 249–263. https://doi.org/10.1080/13603121003692967
6. Peraturan Pemerintah, R. I. Peraturan Pemerintah R.I Nomor 53 Tahun 2010 Tentang Disiplin Pegawai Negeri Sipil, Pub. L. Nomor 53 Tahun 2010, 95 (2010). Jakarta. Retrieved from

http://www.batan.go.id/prod_hukum/extern/pp53.pdf

7. Rahimi, M., & Karkami, F. H. (2015). The role of teachers' classroom discipline in their teaching effectiveness and students' language learning motivation and achievement: A path method. *Iranian Journal of Language Teaching Research*, *3*(1), 57–82. Retrieved from www.urmia.ac.ir/ijltr

8. Rahman, A. (2014). Peningkatan disiplin kerja guru di sekolah dasar yayasan mutiara gambut. *Jurnal Administrasi Pendidikan*, *2*, 1–9. Retrieved from http://ejournal.unp.ac.id/index.php/bahana/article/view/3695/2932

9. Shih, C.-L., Wu, C.-C., Lai, F.-P., & Liao, C.-W. (2015). The Study of Teachers' Attitudes of Positive Disciplines and Class Management Effectiveness in Junior High School. *International Journal of Information and Education Technology*, *5*(7), 507–511. https://doi.org/10.7763/IJIET.2015.V5.558

10. Stanley, E. O. (2014). Discipline and Academic Performance (A Study of Selected secondary Schools in Lagos, Nigeria). *International Journal of Academic Research in Progressive Education and Development*, *3*(1), 181–194. https://doi.org/10.6007/IJARPED/v3-i1/758

11. Sugiyono. (2016). *Statistika untuk Penelitian*. Bandung: Alfabeta

12. Sukmadinata, NS. (2013). Metode Penelitian Pendidikan. Bandung: Rosdakarya

13. Susanty, A., & Baskoro, S. W. (2012). Pengaruh Motivasi Kerja dan Gaya Kepemimpinan Terhadap Disiplin Kerja Serta Dampaknya Pada Kinerja Karyawan (Studi Kasus Pada PT. PLN (Persero) APD Semarang). *Jati UNDIP*, *7*(2), 77–84.

14. Undang-undang Nomor 20 Tahun 2003. (2012). Undang-Undang Republik Indonesia Nomor 20 Tahun 2003 Tentang Sistem Pendidikan Nasional. *Uma Ética Para Quantos?*, *XXXIII*(2), 81–87. https://doi.org/10.1007/s13398-014-0173-7.2

15. Walters, J., & Frei, S. (2007). *Managing Classroom Behavior and Discipline. Oceanus.*

16. Wuryandani, W., Maftuh, B., & Budimansyah, D. (2014). Pendidikan Karakter Disiplin Sekolah Dasar. *Cakrawala Pendidikan*, *33*(2), 286–295. Retrieved from https://journal.uny.ac.id/index.php/cp/article/view/2168

Integrating information technology into Indonesian EFL curriculum

Roro Dewi Wahyu Mustikasari [1], and *Norwanto* Norwanto[2,*]

[1] Institut Agama Islam Negeri (STAIN) Salatiga, Indonesia
[2] Institut Agama Islam Negeri (STAIN) Salatiga, Indonesia

Abstract. Technology-assisted language learning needs to be integrated in curriculum. There are several studies on the usage of technology can be used to improve students' language skills. However, there is significant gap on how to integrate technology into EFL curriculum. This current study focused on how the heads of English Education Department manage the integration of technology into the curriculum, what the steps taken by them to make the integration of technology reliable to be applied into the classroom are, and how the students' attitudes toward the technology integration are. Moreover, it was a descriptive qualitative study using interview to collect the data. The findings showed that (1) the heads of the departments got positive support from institutional policy to integrate technology in their curriculum; (2) there were various steps taken to promote this technology integration; and (3) several students' attitudes can be performed when they joined classes applying technology. It can be concluded that students preferred a blended-learning model.

1 Introduction

A curriculum review is a multifaceted process, which determines curriculum planners to consider present and future educational needs. Toffler [1] claims that curriculum designers need to develop well-organized curricula in order to avoid regular conflict that may occur continuously because they create a new permanent curriculum for all purposes. However, he suggests that sets of impermanent curricula, which have a series of procedure of evaluation and renovation for several years is vital to be developed. His fore coming future shock vision seems it is a real condition nowadays. Curriculum designers experience challenges to review curriculum because they appear to jot down a permanent curriculum, instead of impermanent curricula. Thus reviewing a curriculum demands curriculum planners to have a comprehensive perspective toward old and new changes in educational area.

This present study will not discuss how heads of English education department and teams figure out curriculum review. Instead, new educational changes act as trigger to be considered for curriculum review. Currently, the new common topic, i.e. technology for English teaching and learning process, is prominent topic among educators. Moreover, sustaining professional teaching development using technology is also commonly applied. For example, a tailored made project designed by RELO US Embassy in Indonesia gives a terrific benchmark for professional teaching development using technology. The project called Indonesian Massive Open Online Course (IMOOC), which equips pre-service and in-service English teachers to develop their teaching skills using technology for autonomous learning. It was started in 2017, 15 IMOOC developers (from 15 universities across Indonesia) developed IMOOC to meet Indonesian curriculum. The first year success result is continued with the next session of IMOOC in 2018. It is expected that it can gain another success after reviewing the modules in the first session (this information is gather from an interview with several IMOOC facilitators).

On the other hand, several researchers also marked this phenomenon by conducting researches related to using technology into EFL classrooms. Regarding this study, five previous studies [2 - 5] are used to define the implementations of technology-assisted language learning.

First, Hui et.al [2] conducted the longitudinal experiment study, which intrigued to see the differences between technology-assisted learning and face-to-face learning. The respondents were first-year students at a major university in Hong Kong, and took the mandatory freshman English class. It was found that the students' acquisition of abstract conceptualization and reflective observation were increased when they joined the technology-assisted learning group. In contrast, they indicated to have negative performances for concrete experience. In addition, technology-assisted learning (compared to face-to-face learning) frequently supported vocabulary learning. However, it is less effective to develop the students' listening comprehension skills.

Second, Golonka et.al [3] stated that over 350 published studies (including classroom-based

* Corresponding author: norwanto@iainsalatiga.ac.id

technologies, individual study tools, network-based social computing, and mobile and portable devices) were examined to see effectiveness of using technology in foreign language (FL) learning and teaching. The empirical studies found that the automatic speech recognition (ASR) as the part of the computer-assisted pronunciation training was able to give influence on pronunciation and supply effective feedback. In addition, the use of chat in FL learning showed that significant improvement was captured from the language production of the students.

Third, Toetenel [4] conducted a study on 30 students of a further education in United Kingdom, who joined a social networking site called Ning (she developed it as an open educational resource/ OER). She analyzed their peer interaction in and outside classroom and examined their preference of the type of activities used and effect of these on peer interaction within the research. The results showed that Ning enhanced group cohesion, and the students worked in different groups when they were interacted both in and outside classroom. She found that technical and administrative issue (e.g. IT department was not followed the project even though she got the permission for head of department) as the barriers. In addition, she asserted that the further education college where she conducted her research project did not have policy in term of the use of OER in the classroom.

Fourth, Huang and Chuang [5] investigated the effectiveness of technology-assisted sheltered model by using the animation design course, which adopted content-based instruction (CBI), aimed to boost the students' reading abilities, and implemented in English majors at a technology university in Taiwan. Moreover, there were a control group and an experimental group that consisted of 117 and 121 students respectively. The quantitative and qualitative data revealed significant improvement in the experimental group. The researchers reported this group to have better performances of reading comprehension, reading speed, acceptance, attention, exams, and easing teaching difficulties. Furthermore, the empirical results showed that the technology-assisted sheltered model was generated for EFL multi-purpose courses.

Fifth, Yusny and Kumita [6] found that teaching grammar utilizing Prezi presentation helps students improving their grammar mastery. Thus, it is another evidence that technology influence students' competence.

Mostly all researchers highlight that the integration of technology brings positive improvement for the students' language acquisition. Hui et.al. [2] and Huang and Chuang [5] argue that it has benefits for English skills whereas Golonka et.al [3] mention that it gives valuable effect on FL learning in general. In contrast, Toetenel [4] claims that negative responses of working place in implementing OER in term of the social networking site give technical and administrative obstacles. However, none of the researchers investigates how to integrate technology into curriculum. They frequently only report technology assisted-language learning may influence the students' competence. Therefore, this present study explores technology integration into Indonesian EFL curriculum. It only focuses on curriculum of English Education Departments which organized by Ministry of Religious Affairs of the Republic of Indonesia. In addition, Indonesian EFL curriculum for tertiary schools should be based on National Qualification Framework of Indonesia (*Kerangka Kualifikasi Nasional Indonesia (KKNI)).* It is a standardized Indonesian criterion of learning outcomes that must be achieved by undergraduate students. Thus, it is also interesting to recognize how curriculum designers link *KKNI* toward the curriculum.

1.1 Theoretical framework

Reviewing a curriculum demands curriculum designers to accommodate requested requirements from three fundamental aspects namely learners, teachers, and school. It is a complex situation because it is aimed to comprise present and long-term objectives, which include those required necessities from three fundamental aspects. Richards [7] states that understanding current and long-standing needs of students and society is essential considerations mainly addressed by curriculum planners with regards to develop goal for educational programs. Planners' belief and ideologies about schools, students, and teachers are several factors that reflect how they view learning objectives of educational programs. Thus it seems that learning objectives work in line with prominent requirements that should be mentioned in a curriculum. Currently, technology is one of the requirements that should be addressed in Indonesian EFL curriculum. However, according to Corder and U-Mackey [8], the integration of technology and curriculum must be addressed carefully, to realize the affordances of technology, and linked clearly to learning outcomes and learning, teaching, and assessment activities. In other words, technology must be integrated to resolve pedagogical issues. Although it is important to use technology-assisted language learning, curriculum planners must think about the flexibility and affordability of technology. Another main issue is how to link it into teaching and learning process that associates with learning outcomes and assessment. Therefore, technology integration is suggested to facilitate pedagogical issues rather than it only focuses on digital literacy.

Martin and Grudziecki as quoted by Goodfellow [9] define "digital literacy as the awareness, attitude and ability of individuals to use digital tools for communication, expression and social action in specific life situations." Digital literacy tends to display learners' competence to operate different digital gadgets, which can be used for communication and interaction virtually. Therefore, he asserts that the exemplifications of digital literary are information and communications technology (ICT), technology, information, media, visual and communications literacy [9]. It is described that digital literacy explores digital tools that can be used for communication and interaction, thus, it can be recommended for technology-assisted language learning.

Computer is a very common device that can be used to perform technology-assisted language learning. Although computer assisted language learning (CALL) is a well-known concept among educators, it should not be recognized because it has series of historical phases. Motteram [10] claims that CALL should not be discussed merely regarding to its development historical phases. However, implementing technology into practical usage in classrooms must be explored further in order to shape its benefits for students' learning outcomes. She thinks that students' learning outcomes are more central to be observed because integrating technology into curriculum expects teachers to be reliable to link it into syllabus and course plans. For example, CALL activities can perform computer learner interactions, and all students in a class can actively participate in that interactions in the same time [15]. Thus, it can be assumed that a school must be equipped with computer laboratory. In addition, probably students may provide their personal laptops. It must be highlighted that for this type of CALL activities computer or laptop must be available. Furthermore, CALL activities should focus on the curriculum of English. Chapelle [11] argues that language learning features should be considered as principle of evaluating CALL, as a consequence, language focus should be stated as one of part of CALL tasks. However, Mustikasari [12] says that designing activities for MOOC must avoid a time consuming pattern of learning.

Activities and tasks, which employ technology, become more interesting when e-learning occurs to change face-to-face interaction in a classroom. Coryell and Chlup [13] point out that computer-mediated communication (CMC), language acquisition software, course management software (e.g. WebCT, Moodle, and Blackboard), online streaming audio and video, Internet language learning meeting places (i.e. Dave's ESL Cafe') are various options of e-learning. Moreover, Elliot [14] adds that CMC relies on communication experiences, which use networked computers. CMC can be classified into synchronous (a real time event) such as instant messaging, video conferencing; and asynchronous namely email, internet forums. Those online learning activities utilize virtual communication in order to invite students to use English in real-life situation. Coryell and Chlup [13] suggest four characteristics of e-learning activities which are taken from the survey and focus group discussion data in implementing e-learning for adult English language learners, namely preparation, individualized, student-centered instruction, support, and collaboration. Those features are expected to maximize students' independent learning.

On the other hand, blended learning emerges to be preferred. Hubackovaa [15] asserts that blended learning will be frequently used in the future because her survey result reveals that among adults students from lifelong education from divergent types of school are indicated to used blended learning as their preference. Blended learning is also well-known as "hybrid learning" [16] and it is probably liked by adult students because it is a combination of face-to-face and online learning.

Both of e-learning and blended learning demand teachers to have a well-structured preparation to design them. Compton [17] claims some aspects needed to be adjusted to prepare language teachers to teach language online:

1) Despite of technical and software specific skills (which can be learned), online language teachers should spend more time on how to develop their skills to facilitate online socializing and community building for students so that meaningful communicative interaction can be boosted
2) A language teacher education program should be framed for three categories of online language teaching skills (technology, pedagogy and evaluation) which accommodate three levels of expertise (novice, proficient and expert)
3) Divergent roles and responsibilities of online language teachers in the online language learning system must be recognized in order to avoid gaps and take necessary actions.
4) Learning system concerning integration of online language teaching and learning must be related to issues in existing curriculum design and methods courses.

From his perspectives, it can be defined that teachers must recognize their personal competence to teach online because each teacher has unalike levels of expertise. Similar to Compton, Hanson [18] adds that educators can be categorized into two big domains namely innovators (those who are able to take a risk by trying new ideas that use latest technology and desiring for revolutionary change) and majority (those who need help, opportunity, and confidence to try ICT for teaching). Both classifications of teachers' technological competence are important to be noticed because technical issues are needed to solve. In addition, teachers can learn how to use software and other technology specific skills; as a result, they can provide a virtual interaction, which is meaningful and communicative. Therefore, it is crucial to set up standard of operational procedure of those members of online learning facilitator. On the other hand, integration of online activities, which is suitable with current curriculum and course is another vital issue. Technology-assisted language learning should address language pedagogy because students' language competence must be concerned first in order to maximize their learning outcomes.

Students' learning outcomes must be stated in a curriculum; therefore, curriculum designers need to arrange an intended learning outcome. Biggs and Tang [19] offer three levels of outcome statements of intended learning outcome, they are (1) institutional level (a statement of competence of a university graduation), (2) program level (a statement of competence of a department graduation), and (3) course level (a statement of competence of a course completion). An interconnection among those levels must be smoothly organized so that an intended learning outcome is reliable to be jotted down and achieved.

An intended learning outcome should facilitate students to perform their learning process rather than learning product. A learning process resembles students' learning experiences. For instance, CBI is adopted in a curriculum. CBI supplies authentic content that it can be used to contextualize learning in order to foster dual learning that is language and content [5]. Therefore, students' learning experience must be facilitated with activities that explore authentic materials' usage, and both language-driven and content-driven should be linked and mentioned in an intended learning outcome that wisely addresses learning process compared to learning product. It is expected that students can show their independent learning. Papadima-Sophocleous [20] informs that autonomous learning is frequently occurred in an integral element of language education in Cyprus. It can be systematically designed because it is aimed to foster the students to perform their autonomous language learning, to provide effective learning potential, to boost lifelong language learning, and to shape European intercultural awareness and communication identity. Regarding to enhance independent learning, some actions are taken such as maximizing the school library programs, sustaining the language rooms, and promoting new syllabuses. This is a good example of how to design a curriculum, which includes all requirements that considered the need of schools, teachers, and students. In contrast, other scholars mention another students' personal behavior, which can be reported to influence students' independent learning in language learning using technology. Lai and Gu [21] state that some factors of the students' self-regulations such as goal commitment, resource, affection, culture learning, metacognition, and social connection regulation respectively influence Hong Kong university students' careful choices of technology for language learning. They also mention that the students' perspective on language training is not merely vital in language learning beliefs. In addition, they also show their point of view in technology-assisted language learning which it is a reflection of their metacognitive knowledge. It can be clearly recognized that both of behaviors, autonomous learning and self-regulations can be used to enhance students' language learning using technology. Thus in this study, I will pursue to investigate how the heads of English Education Department manage the integration of technology into the curriculum, what steps they do to integrate technology into classrooms, and how the students' attitudes toward the technology integration are.

2 Methods

This study was a descriptive qualitative study. Larsen-Freeman and Long [22] state that Qualitative paradigm has some attributes such as it is "process-oriented; valid, rich, deep data; holistic; natural; subjective; dynamic reality; descriptive; exploratory, etc." Thus, this study tried to find out the general implementation of the integration of technology into the Indonesian EFL curriculum.

The locations of study were 11 English education departments of the state Islamic tertiary educations (i.e. universities and institutes), which are located on western Indonesian time zone. They are managed by Ministry of Religious Affairs of the Republic of Indonesia. In the first step, the researchers interviewed 11 heads of the departments who are the members of the committee of the English Linguistics Literature and Education (ELITE). It is a national-based association of English lecturers. The interview was conducted to gain initial information about the use of technology in the 11 English education departments. The second step was in-depth interview. The participants were 5 of the 11 head departments, who has applied blended learning. The five departments has qualified for level of A or B for the department accreditation.

2.1. Data collection

Firstly, open-ended interview was proceeded to gain the data. Three IMOOC facilitators examined and validated the list of interview questions. McKay [23] claims that an open-ended interview provides a well-constructed standard of procedure because it has specified questions that have the same order and exact words so that identical questions are given to participants. Thus, comparable data and data analysis are easier to do. Secondly, curriculum, lesson plan, and departments' academic information on websites were needed as documents.

2.2 Data analysis

The data was analyzed with deductive approach. Coding, classifying and categorizing the data were done. Baralt [24] states that some features of qualitative coding are: (1) including series of reading and examining data, (2) using extracting themes of data as initial steps of coding, (3) comparing themes from some data types, therefore, this present study compared the data from interview and documentation.

3 Findings and discussion

The findings and discussion are separately presented in the following sections.

3.1 The heads of English education departments manage the integration of technology into the curriculum

The institutional and faculty policy played a vital role to shape the departments' curriculum. This was the basic base for the departments to make legal steps regarding their initiatives toward new changes that influenced by the trend in education and stakeholders' requirements for the qualified-alumnae. The departments' initiatives also supported and facilitated by the institutional positive regulation of infrastructure toward the usage of technology in equipping academic and administrative atmospheres.

Each university and institution has online integrated-system for academic and administrative matters. Particularly for academic needs, this system utilizes such as blog staff and e-learning. Lecturers might upload their teaching documents (syllabus, course plan, teaching material) in blog staff. On the other hand, lecturers could have online class using e-learning portal. However, it found that most of the heads of department mentions that blog staff and e-learning were not used effectively by lecturers because lecturers tended to use face-to-face meeting rather than online meeting. In contrast, there was only 1 university confirmed that lecturers must do online meeting, eventough, they had to simply inform only assignments in the online integrated academic system which provides some features namely home, profile, students' academic assistance, grade, schedule, electronic syllabus. This online system facilitates lecturers to upload and text their assignments. Moreover, students had an out-class activity to learn and do assignments. Thus, it seemed that this university had a blended-learning environment. In addition, the institutional policy did not have a strict rule of how many percentages in arranging the combination of face-to-face and online meeting that must be done by lecturers. A design for fashion time allocation to organize blended-learning were mandatory for lecturers.

The institutional and faculty policy as well as the infrastructure were strengthening the heads of the departments to arrange the well-organized curriculum. Based on the data, all heads of department and teams had the adequate ability to integrate technology into their curriculum.

They organized the curriculum based on *KKNI,* which is used to standardized criterion of targeted-learning outcomes for undergraduate alumnae. This stage was the starting point for them to design the set of departments' curriculum identities namely the vision, mission, goal, targeted-learning outcomes and a milestone of specific strategy. It can be reported that the identities of the departments' curriculum had a friendly concepts, which display various efforts to accommodate the integration of technology into the curriculum. Following the education trends on the usage of technology for language learning and supplying the requests from the stakeholders in the needs of qualified alumnae are crucial factors, which influence the heads and teams to integrate technology for their curriculum.

Regarding one of the essential components of the specific-skills of Level 6 for undergraduate alumnae in *KKNI*, it is stated and translated that undergraduate alumnae has the ability of specific skills to use the technology to teach and do research in English teaching. Therefore, the heads of the departments and teams used this component to make a remarkable act of integrating technology toward the curriculum. Several initialing acts that can be informed as follows:

1. Discuss and state the identities of the departments which utilize technology
2. Choose subjects of study that contain technology-based assisted language learning
3. Illuminate the syllabus of the subjects
4. Organize course plan

Moreover, related evidence toward the above acts was found, they were:

1. Majority of the departments' curriculum identities had stated the term "information and communication technology, information technology, or technology"
2. The subjects, which implemented the technology-based assisted language learning (the subjects were gather across the departments; the same subjects' names are not repeated) are Integrating ICT in Curriculum and Instruction (elective), EFL Instruction with Multimedia, ELT Media Design, EFL Pedagogies for Flexible Learning, Computer-Assisted Language Learning (CALL), English course design, Instructional Media, Media Instructional Technology, Internet-based Language Teaching, Macro Media Flash, Instructional Material and Media Development, Media for Teaching Young Learners (elective)
3. The course plan, which elaborated syllabus, clearly defined the topics of discussion that address technology enhancing English language teaching. Moreover, lecturers have the chance to initiate new topics of discussion in their course plan; however, they have to relate new topics with the syllabus. The course plan provides sufficient knowledge for students of how to integrate technology into classroom activities when they act as teachers. For example, from the data, it was appeared that the course plan of the same name of subject can have different topics; nevertheless, it had ample coverage topics on specific virtual learning environment platform, related software, and websites, virtual ethnicity, technology in education, history of CALL, and online resources for English as foreign language teachers.

3.2 The steps taken by the heads of the departments to make the integration of technology reliable to be applied into the classroom activities

After structuring the curriculum document, the heads of departments tried to manage and facilitate lecturers to have a better performance in teaching using technology. Four steps were taken in integrating technology to be more feasible in the teaching and learning process: 1) providing supportive department policy, 2) conducting workshop, 3) organizing equipments/ tools, 4) having regular supervision system.

Majority of the heads of the department did not have firm rule toward department policy using technology in the classroom. Lecturers were freely taught using technology as their wish. In contrast, there was only 1 head of department that assigned lecturers to teach at least 1 subject using a blended-learning environment, and he had a special workshop to assist lecturers so that his effort was realistic to be done. He asked 1 lecturer to train the other lecturers using canvas.instructure as the platform for blended-learning.

On the other hand, all heads of department organize several workshops that can be used to give insight for lecturers regarding the implementation of technology into their daily classroom activities. In addition, budgeting for lecturers' trainings came from the institution, faculty or department schemes. On the contrary, the heads of department might organize non-budgeting workshop which commonly recognized as lecturer discussion forum, and it is a monthly meeting. Nevertheless, the topics of discussion could be various because they depended on lecturers' preferences who present their talks. Another way to furnish lecturers digital literacy, the heads of the department assigned certain lecturers to follow workshops that organized by RELO US Embassy and AUSAID. The lecturers who were mandated to join this teacher training programs trained the other colleagues after they finished the programs. Moreover, the data showed that there was 1 department which had approximately 6 lecturers who act as trainers for teacher professional development for external audiences.

Besides facilitated lecturers with workshops, providing equipments/ tools also became an issue to be considered. The term equipments/ tools refer to infrastructures and technology resources. The former items could be best seen from computer laboratory, smart classrooms which have LCD projector and wifi. Each department had those items. Furthermore, bring-your-own laptop/ gadget policy tended to be arranged and agreed between lecturers and students. While technology recourses might be founded in the usage of platform, software, and social media. The platform were canvas.instructure, moodle, Google classroom, Google form, email. Then there were several common software: PeerWise, camtasia, storyline2, edmodo, and Rosseta Stone. Meanwhile, facebook and instagram were famous social media. From the above data, it can be inferred that all departments used both types of CMC: 1) synchronous (a real time event namely social media), 2) asynchronous (such as email, and the above platform as the internet forum).

Although lecturers were reported to use the above platform, software, and social media, the heads of the departments had a system of customary supervision. It was normally done for twice per semester, and it was held in the mid-term and final-term. Basically, the system was not creating to address technology requirements in the teaching process; however, it covered all teaching aspects. In addition, students were examined lecturers' teaching performances by using online and printed form. The results of the assessments were informed to lecturers, and the heads of departments kept the confidential identity of the students.

Even though most of the heads of the department realized that lecturers probably did not use technology to teach for some reasons as follow:

1) They were senior who were not tech-savvy lecturers
2) The subject of study did not need to be delivered using technology

In contrast, disagreement to the above reasons was mentioned by 1 head of department. He said that age was not the main problem why the senior could not do teaching using technology. They were able to integrate technology in their classroom if they get a series of workshop, however, it might take a longer time to be fluent using technology. Therefore, he assigned a tech-savvy lecturer to organize helpdesk. Those steps that were crucial to help lecturers to teach using technology.

Another phenomenon arising in this study is that the heads of the departments considered CBI for non-English classes. English lecturers had the ability to teach non-English subject such as English for Islamic Studies, Education Management, Learning Theories, Philosophy in Education, English for Tourism, English for Business, Contemporary Issues in Islamic Studies, Introduction to Entrepreneurship, Islamic Entrepreneurship, English for Tourism, English for Correspondence, and English for Journalistic. Moreover, the result found that they also used technology in the process of teaching.

3.3 The students' attitudes toward the technology integration

Engage and active students were informed to be appeared when they attended the classes that employ technology as their learning activities. Thus, student-centered paradigm tended to be facilitated by lecturers. Another attitude, which dominantly display by students when they joined a blended-learning environment was autonomous learning. They felt excited with the new learning concept. In addition, lecturers who teach the subjects provided helpdesk. An interesting situation also appeared in providing helpdesk for the students. The helpdesk was organized by English students association from 1 university. The head of department asserted that the students have a solid skillful team so that they are able to help their friends whenever they have obstacles to use technology.

3.4 Discussion

The long process of integrating technology into the curriculum needs to be assisted from the top to bottom level. The departments will not able to have a legalized-curriculum which integrate technology if they do not have supportive encouragement and facilitation from the university or institution. As a result, the alumnae learning outcomes can meet stakeholders' expectation.

A series of workshop to boost lecturers' intention to teach using technology will need to be maintained the future so that no more senior will be labeled as non tech-savvy lecturers. From the data revealed that majority of lecturers tended to have low until medium skills of using technology. Working with the students to have the helpdesk is also interesting to be proceeded because it will foster scaffolding that can bring positive effect to minimize students' problems in using technology.

Technology assisted-language learning is emerged to have a blended-learning environment as the preference among the departments. This type of learning can be used to accommodate the students with virtual learning environment as well as face-to-face meetingside.

4 Conclusion

The findings of this current study basically support Bach, et.al (2007). Their idea of blended-learning is preferable among adult learners is proof in this study. It is true that they like the activities of learning that combine online and face-to-face meeting. Recommendation for future study will be very useful to investigate the model of blended-learning which employ scaffolding between students to boost autonomous learning and self-regulated learning

References

1. A. Toffler, *Future Shock,* (Random House, Inc., New York, 1970)
2. W. Hui, P. J. H. Hu, T. H. K. Clark, K. Y. Tam, J. Milton, *Journal of Computer Assisted Learning*, **24**, (2008)
3. E. M. Golonkaa, A. R. Bowlesa, V. M. Franka, D. L. Richardson, S. Freynika, *Computer Assisted Language Learning*, **2**, 1, (2014)
4. L. Toetenel, *Computer Assisted Language Learning*, **27**, 2, (2014)
5. Y. H. Huang, T. Y. Chuang, *Computer Assisted Language Learning*, **29**, 3, (2016)
6. Rahmat Yusni, Desi Nanda Kumita, *Englisia,* **3**, 2, (2016)
7. J. C. Richards, *Curriculum Development in Language Teaching*, (Cambridge University Press, Cambridge, 2001)
8. D, Corder, A, U-Mackey, Integration of Technology for Effective Learning, Teaching, and Assessment in M. Levy, F. Blin, C. B. Siskin, O. Takeuchi, (eds), *World CALL International Perspectives on Computer-Assisted Language Learning,* (Routlegde, New York , 2011)
9. R. Goodfellow, *Teaching in Higher Education*, **16**, 1, (2011)
10. G. Motteram, Developing and Extending our Understanding of Language Learning and Technology in G. Motteram, (ed), *Innovations in Learning Technologies for English Language Teaching,* (British Council, 2013)
11. Carol Chapelle, *Computer Applications in Second Language Acquisition: Foundations for Teaching, Testing and Research* (Cambridge University Press, Cambridge, 2001)
12. Dewi W. Mustikasari, *Register Journal*, **10**, 2, (2017)
13. J. E. Coryell, D. T. Chlup, *Computer Assisted Language Learning*. **20**, 3, (2007)
14. D. Elliott, Internet Technologies and Language Teacher Education in Michael Thomas, (ed) *Handbook of Research on Web 2.0 and Second Language Learning*, (Information Science Reference, New York, 2009)
15. S. Hubackovaa, *Procedia-Social and Behavioral Sciences,* **197**, (2015)
16. S. Bach, P. Haynes, J.L. Smith, *Online Learning and Teaching in Higher Education,* (McGraw-Hill Companies, Berkshire, 2007)
17. L. K. L. Compton, *Computer Assisted Language Learning*, **22**, 1, (2009)
18. J. Hanson, *Staff Development for ICT and E-Learning: Skills or Pedagogy?* (www.ltsn.ac.uk/genericcentre, 2002)
19. J. Biggs, C.Tang, *Teaching for Quality Learning at University* (McGraw-Hill Companies, Berkshire, 2007)
20. S. Papadima-Sophocleous, Electronic Portfolios in a BA CALL Course Supporting Reflective and Autonomous Learning in M. Levy, F. Blin, C. B. Siskin, O. Takeuchi, (eds.), *World CALL International Perspectives on Computer-Assisted Language Learning,* (Routlegde, New York, 2011)
21. C. Lai, M. Gu, *Computer Assisted Language Learning*, **24**, 4, (2011)
22. D. Larsen-Freeman, M. H. Long, *An Introduction to Second Language Acquisition Research*, (Taylor & Francis, New York, 1991)
23. S. L. McKay, *Researching Second Language Classrooms,* (Lawrence Erlbaum Associates, Inc., New Jersey, 2006)
24. M. Baralt, Coding Qualitative Data in A. Mackey, S. Gass, (eds), *Research Methods in Second Language Acquisition: A Practical Guide,* (Blackwell Publishing Ltd., West Sussex, 2012)

The Use of Ipad in Learning Islamic Religion Education at the Eighth Graders of Sabilurrasyad Junior High School, Bojong Ngampel Kendal

Muzdalifah[1,*], *Sri* Wahyuningsih[2], and *Muhammad* Mashuri[3]

[1]State Institution of Islamic Studies (IAIN) Kudus, Islamic Religion Department, Conge Ngembalrejo Street,51 Kudus, Indonesia
[2] State Institution of Islamic Studies (IAIN) Kudus, English Department, Conge Ngembalrejo Street, 51 Kudus, Indonesia
3 State Institution of Islamic Studies (IAIN) Kudus, Islamic Religion Department, Conge Ngembalrejo Street,51 Kudus, Indonesia

Abstract. This study aims at finding the use of Ipad in learning Islamic Religion Education at the eighth graders of Sabilurrasyad Junior High school, Bojong Ngampel Kendal.This study used a qualitative research method. Data were gathered through an observation, indepth-interview and documentation. The results of this study indicate that the use of Media of Ipad Learning in Islamic Religion Education Class at the eighth graders of Sabilurrasyad Junior High School, Bojong Ngampel Kendal is considered effective. Furthermore, the average value of Islamic religion education after the implementation of Ipad media is higher that is 85.67 compared to the previous one 81.14. The supporting factors of the Ipad media are the internet network provided by the school, training from the Information Technology Development Agency, Ipad interestingly attracts students' attention and motivation, iPad can present material in audio visual form. Meanwhile, the inhibiting factors of using ipad are limited battery power or usage, unstable internet network, students' lack of knowledge in using ipad, and there is no filter to block inappropriate sites.

Keywords: *Ipad, Islamic Religion Education, Sabilurrasyad Junior High School*

1. Introduction

The development of globalization era is clearly indicated by the advancement of science and technology, especially in the field of information and communication technology which increasingly shows its development. The advancement of technology nowadays especially in the field of information and communication causes the narrower world in scope, for instance, the interaction between one nation to others both intentionally and unintentionally become more intensive. (Darmawan, 2012: 7-8). Information and communication technology is growing rapidly with various forms and interests that are widespread throughout the world. Indeed, technological and communication progress can be considered as the spread and intensification of economic, social and cultural relations that penetrate the geographical barriers of space and time that occur in various fields of life such as ideology, politics, economics, social and especially in the field of education.

The influence of the development of information and communication technology in the world of education is very large, particluarly in the shift of education paradigm. This occurs due to corrections, changes, and new studies that have influenced the development of concepts and praxis in the education system (Abdulhaq, 2015: 1). This change should be considered by practitioners of education, where educational activities must also be adapted to the times, no longer using the conventional and monotonous education system, which has been running recently. This paradigm should be changed that the conventional education system is gradually shifted towards a modern education system. In this case, teachers should be active in teaching and learning activities. However, students are also required to actively seek information independently from various sources such as books, internet and others by utilizing the available technology.

In the National Education System Law, it is explained that a national education is based on the Pancasila and the 1945 Constitution which is based on religious values, Indonesian national culture and responsive to the demands of changing times (UURI, 2007: 3-4). The use of information technology (Information Technology) in the field of education is an effort to find the solution to answer all the challenges. Information technology (IT) is a supporter of institutional capabilities, including educational institutions (Asmani, J.M. (2011: 7). Various aspects behind the development of technology, especially information technology are deep involvement in its application (Hadisi et al, 2015: 120).

The previous study on the effect of the use of Internet-based learning information technology on Islamic Religion Education learning interest in the grade students of SMP N 30 Semarang in Academic Year 2011/2012 found that the use of information technology

* Corresponding author: Muzdalifah@stainkudus.ac.id

on Internet-based learning has a significant influence on learning interest of PAI students of eight grade at SMP N 30 Semarang (Nurfahmi, 2012). In addition, information technology-based learning to improve motivation and achievement learning morals of eight grade students at State Islamic Junior High School semanu gunungkidul yogyakarta. The results of the study explain that information technology-based morality learning can improve the learning motivation of the eight grade students at MTsN Semanu. These include positive changes in students' behavior during the learning process, pleasure and high entusiasm in learning process(Athoillah, 2012).

From the research above it can be concluded that educational institutions are needed so that they can be realized. Educational institutions must be active, creative and productive in reading this latest phenomenon. One of the ways is to design a grand design as a foundation for advancing information and communication technology (Asmani, 2011: 7). Students should not miss information, school facilities and infrastructure must be equipped, the spirit to try new things should be encouraged, and work activities should continue to be fostered optimally.

Junior high school of Sabilurrasyad Bojong Ngampel Kendal as a private formal education institution was established two years ago. In accordance with it, this school has the responsibility to become muslim students. It has become the goal of Islamic education and also has deep knowledge and the ability to master technology that is currently showing such rapid development. To achieve this, the school offers one program, in which the students are expected to master the technology that will be used in the learning process so that students not only master the subject matter, but also the information and communication technology.

In the learning process of iPad or i-learning at Sabilurrasyad Junior High School, Bojong Ngampel Kendal, each teacher and student is given one iPad. The teachers call this kind of learning as "One Teacher One Tab and One Student One Tab". This means that when learning takes place, one teacher is given one ipad and one student is also given one ipad as a medium in the implementation of teaching and learning activities (Ghofur, August, 2016). This learning is a new breakthrough that unites learning, playing and working, so the realization of learning is integrated with all aspects of life through this ipad media. Everything is packaged simply to facilitate students in developing creativity and critical thinking. This article aims to explain the application of IT (Information Technology) based Islamic Religion learning through the Ipad Learning media at Sabilurrasyad Junior High School Bojong Ngampel Kendal and the learning outcomes of grade VIII students after the implementation of IT (Information Technology) in learning the Islamic education through Ipad Learning media as well as supporting and inhibiting factors for the application of IT (Information Technology) based PAI learning in the eighth grade students.

2. METHODS

This study belongs to a descriptive qualitative research. The data are obtained through observation, In-depth interviews to the principal, teachers and eighth grade students of Islamic Junior High School Sabilurrasyad Bojong Ngampel Kendal and documentation that is in accordance with the needs of research data at Sabilurrasyad Islamic Junior High School Bojong Ngampel Kendal.

3. Literatures Review

3.1. Basic Islamic Education Learning in Junior High School

In activities that are sustainable as a transformation of science, education requires a strong foundation. The basis surely is based on Islamic education. This is viewed from three aspects, namely legal, religious and psychological social basis (Alim, 2006: 4). The juridical or legal basis is the basis for the implementation of religious education derived from legislation that can indirectly become a guide in carrying out formal religious education in schools. In addition, the basis of religious PAI learning is based on the Qur'an and Hadith, among others (Q.S. An-Nahl / 16: 125), namely:

ادْعُ إِلى سَبِيْلِ رَبِّكَ بِالحِكْمَةِ وَالمَوْعِظَةِ الحَسَنَةِ وَجَادِلْهُم بِالَّتِيْ هِيَ اَحْسَنَ إِنَّ
رَبَّكَ هُوَ اَعْلَمُ بِمَنْ ضَلَّ عَنْ سَبِيْلِهِ صلى وَهُوَ اَعْلَمُ بِالمُهْتَدِيْنَ

Meaning: "Call (humans) to the way of your Lord with good wisdom and lessons and argue them in a good way. Verily your Lord He who knows more about who is lost from His ways, and He who knows better those who get guidance.

Meanwhile, the basis of psychological social assumes that as human social beings, adequate knowledge is needed in accordance with development and culture. However, in essence, among humans, one with the others will never be the same in all matters, including in its degree and position. The social basis for the implementation of Islamic religion learning is in accordance with (Q.S. Al-Hujarat / 49: 13)

ياايها الناس انا خلقنكم من ذكر وانثى وجعلنكم شعوبا وقبائل لتعارفوا ج ان
اكرمكم عند الله اتقكم ج ان الله عليم خبير

Meaning: "O man, Truly We created you from a man and a woman and made you nation - nation and tribe so that you know each other. Surely the noblest person among you on the side of Allah is the one who is the most pious among you. Verily Allah is all-knowing, the All-Knowing

3.2 Scope of Islamic Education in Junior High School

In terms of the content of the Islamic religion education material, it cannot be separated from the three basic frameworks of Islamic teachings, namely: aqidah, syari'ah and akhlak. From the three basic teachings of Islam, various Islamic studies such as fiqh, morality, and other sciences developed based on the object of their respective studies. The scope of learning Islamic Education in Junior High School covers faith, Al Qur'an and Hadith, morals, worship, and history. The point of faith refers to believe to God and the other faith pillars. Therefore, students are taught how to believe to God and the other faith pillars. Indeed, this is the basis of students' confidence in the religion they adhere to.

3.3 Objectives of Learning Islamic Education in Junior High School Colour

Islamic Religious Education in Junior High School aims to develop the faith through giving, fertilizing, and developing knowledge, habituation, and experience of students about Islam so that it becomes a Muslim man who is always faithful and devoted to Allah SWT, realizing a devout and noble Indonesian human being, for developing students' ability to develop, understand and practice the values of Islamic religion, mastery of science, technology and art and to improve intelligence, knowledge, personality, noble character, skills to live independently and follow further education and improve the procedures for reading al -Qur'an and recitation are correct (Depdiknas, 2003: 8).

3.4 Learning with I-Pad Learning Media

Information and Communication Technology (ICT) as part of science and technology in general are all technologies related to the collection, collection, processing, storage, dissemination and presentation of information (Darmawan, 2012:1). In this case, it is certainly related to education. The use of technology in the world of education is a complex and integrated process that involves people, procedures, ideas, equipment and organizations to analyze problems, solve problems, implement, evaluate, and manage problem solving that involves all aspects of student learning (Miarso, 1986 : 1).

I-learning is a means, source and tool to maximize learning potential and to meet the needs of students in mastering learning material effectively and efficiently (Desrianti et al., 2011: 126). The I-learning system is a conventional learning system that is applied in a modern way. Therefore, I-learning is packaged in such a way as to support content. The existence of supporting media in teaching and learning activities will be very beneficial for students including overcoming the limitations of the mind, expanding the imagination, and clarifying abstract things by giving a more realistic picture.

In addition, there are other terms in calling learning with this ipad learning media. "One teacher one tab and one student one tab" the term is used by teaching staff at Sabilurrasyad Bojong Ngampel Kendal Islamic Junior High School on the use of this ipad learning media. In essence, the learning system used is the same as using iPad media, where each teacher and student is given facilities in the form of iPad during. Therefore, the teachers at State Islamic Junior High School Sabilurrasyad Bojong Ngampel Kendal called it the term "One Teacher One Tab and One Student One Tab" (Ghofur, November, 2016).

The purpose of the implementation of the ipad learning media is to build a new I-Tech based Learning System with improvements to the existing system, to change the teaching and learning method with the old system to be a more effective, efficient, paperless and attractive method, and to change the perspective of the teaching staff and students about learning that were previously boring. By using i-learning, the classroom atmosphere will be much more comfortable and enjoyable. The application of four systems (Learning, Playing, Working, Praying) is done simultaneously with only one small tool called iPad (Henderi, 2012: 338).

3.5 Learning Outcomes

In general, learning outcomes can be grouped into three domains, namely cognitive, affective, and psychomotor. These domains cover cognitive domain which have the purpose of education related to intellectual ability or thinking ability, such as the ability to remember and the ability to solve problems. Further, the cognitive domain according to Bloom consists of six levels, namely knowledge, understanding, application, analysis, synthesis, and evaluation.

Affective domain deals with attitudes, values, and appreciation. The type of affective learning outcomes appear in students in various behaviors such as attention to learning, discipline, learning motivation, respect for teachers and classmates, study habits and others. There are five levels in this affective domain, namely acceptance, responding, appreciating, organization, and lifestyle. Moreover, psychomotor domain deals with learning outcomes in the psychomotor field appear in the form of individual skills and acting abilities. There are five levels in this domain, namely imitation, manipulation, precision, articulation, and naturalization (Dimyati, 2009: 201).

4. Results and Discussion

4.1 Implementation of Islamic Religion Education Learning Class In the Eighth Graders Through Ipad Learning at Sabilurrasyad Junior High School in Kendal

Based on the results of interviews with Islamic Religion Education teachers, Khoiriyyah (2017) reveals that the teaching and learning process of the eight grade students using Ipad learning media in Islamic Religion Education, that:

"In Islamic education learning I usually teach with methods that are often used, namely lectures, question and answer, discussions, presentations and so on. From these methods then I combine them with ipad learning media or here commonly called one teacher one tab and one student one tab. But I also adjust to the material I teach, because the use of learning media if it is not adapted to the material will also be in vain. The application of Ipad Learning learning media that I did in class with the following procedure: I set the goal of teaching using learning media, in this step formulating the objectives to be achieved. Then, I prepare the media that will be used, namely ipad learning, before learning I check the material to be taught on the ipad that will be used. Furthermore, students are given directions in advance to be able to use the media to be used namely the ipad. After that the presentation of lessons and demonstrations. There are several forms, some in the form of ibook, in which there are books in the form of files that have been stored on the iPad, there are power point slides, or in the form of videos related to the subject matter. After the preparations are completed, the learning activities are completed. The steps are in accordance with the RPP I made. Then the last step of the lesson evaluation " (Khoiriyyah, August, 2017).

Fig. 1. IPad preparation (checking) before learning through ipad learning media.

As stated by Maswan that there are several steps that can be urdertaken by a teacher in the use of learning media. These steps apply to all types of media used by teachers in the implementation of learning using media. These steps include: First, the teacher sets teaching goals. Second, the teacher sets teachers' preparation. In this phase the teacher prepares the media to be used. Third, the teacher sets class preparation. Students and tecahers should have preparation before learning process. Fourth, the steps for presenting lessons and demonstrations. Fifth, the evaluation (Maswan et al., 2017: 158-159).

The implementation of IT-based Islamic Education learning activities through the Ipad Learning media was also revealed by Ghofur (2018) as the principal stated as follows:

"In PAI learning, the eighth grade Islamic Education maple teacher uses Ipad Learning media which is learning that utilizes ipad in delivering the material taught and combined with other learning methods. In one meeting, Islamic Education map teachers usually combine ipad learning media with other methods that can facilitate the transfer of material to students, such as discussion / presentation methods, or by displaying videos according to the taught material. I think PAI learning using the Ipad Learning learning media is effective because students will be motivated by learning using this ipad, they look active in learning, are also trained to find and bring up ideas and creative solutions in solving problems that match the material taught" (Ghofur, August, 2017).

In the era of globalization, being a teacher is not only limited to standing in front of the class lecturing about the material in the guidebook. Furthermore, the teacher should have various competencies to support the professionalism of the task and its role. One proof of the competence of a teacher is how he is able to guide and create a learning process in order to achieve the competency targets to be achieved. The teacher should know the strategies and learning models that are suitable to be implemented during the teaching and learning process (Shoimin, 2014: 5). To achieve that, a new paradigm is needed by a teacher in the learning process, from the teacher-centered learning to innovative and student-centered learning. These changes begin in terms of curriculum, learning model, or teaching method (Shoimin, 2014: 16).

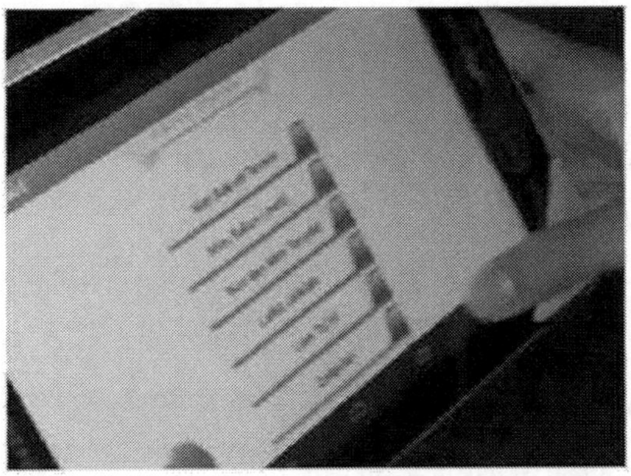

Fig. 2. Form an Ibook containing Islamic Education Materials

The process of teaching and learning activities when using learning Ipad learning media becomes more conducive. Students feel enjoyable and enthusiastic. Additionally, they follow the procedures directed by the teacher in learning. The applied learning does not only affect the smart students, but the whole one feels a positive influence. This is in accordance with the statement delivered by Ula (2017), the eight student at Sabilurrasyad Junior High School Bojong Ngampel Kendal stating that:

"At first I was a little difficult to use it because I only had an iPad, but over time I got used to it because there was an introduction and direction to use it from the teacher. Now, I feel the learning is fun and not boring mas "(Ula, October, 2017).

Teachers are required to have multiple roles so as to create effective and enjoyable learning conditions. Nowadays, most teachers teach using traditional teaching methodologies. The method of teaching is authoritarian and teacher centered. Learning activities are teacher-centered, while students are only used as objects not subjects. The teacher gives lectures to students while students only listen. This causes students to become bored and bored so that it is difficult to receive the material provided by the teacher (Shoimin, 2014: 17).

Based on the observations, it can be concluded that in the process of teaching and learning using the IPad learning media in the eight grade of Sabilurrasyad Junior High School could run well. Students get the attention and show maximum results during teaching and learning process. In addition, learning process carried out will not be monotonous. In this matter, learning becomes effective because it can provoke students to be more active and independent and facilitate students in absorbing learning material.

4.2 Supporting and Inhibiting Factors in the Implementation of Ipad Learning at Sabilurrasyad Junior High School, Bojong Kendal

The results of the interview with Khoiriyyah (2017) show that:

"Supporting factors in the implementation of IT-based PAI learning with Ipad Learning media are: the existence of facilities in the form of ipad and equipped with internet networks provided by schools can support learning, learning materials are available on the ipad so students are very easy to access, Ipad is more attractive the attention and motivation of students rather than using books that they consider boring, Ipad can present material in audio visual form so that it can develop students' thinking skills and understanding, by using an ipad that is connected to the internet network can train students to face and solve actively and creatively problem by digging up information related to the material, using ipad students can easily save the subject matter. While the inhibiting factors of the implementation of IT-based PAI learning with Ipad Learning are: Ipad is an electronic device so it has limited battery power or usage, the internet network is sometimes unstable so that it can make access disrupted, some students cannot use the ipad so it looks passive in participating in learning, there is no filter to block sites that are not suitable for students to access "(Khoiriyah, August, 2017)

In addition, Ghofur (2017) as the principal of Sabilurrasyad Junior High School Bojong Ngampel Kendal explains that there are several factors that could support and inhibit IT-based learning with the Ipad Learning media. This is in accordance with his statement that:

"Supporting factors of IT-based PAI learning with the Ipad Learning media is the training of the Central Java Province Information and Communication Technology Development Agency (BPTIK) which is followed by teachers so that it can be used as a teacher's provision in implementing IT-based learning using ipad, ipad is more attractive attention and learning motivation of students so as to increase student learning passion, Ipad can present material in audio visual form so that it can develop students' thinking and understanding skills. While the inhibiting factor is that we know that ipad is an electronic device that uses batteries so that its usage is limited, lack of supervision from teachers to students so that students sometimes abuse it by accessing sites outside of material and there is no filter to filter inappropriate sites. "(Ghofur, August, 2017).

While the supporting and inhibiting factors experienced by students in the implementation of learning IT through ipad learning media in Islamic Religion Education at Sabilurrasuad Junior High School Bojong Ngampel Kendal are advocated by Saeful (2017) as the eight grade student:

"The supporting factor of the teacher in carrying out the learning process in the classroom is very good and patient towards the students. The lessons presented were packaged using ipad media so it made me interested in taking lessons, and I could understand the material delivered very well. The inhibiting factor is that sometimes the preparation is less like there is an ipad that has not been rolled off so the battery runs out in the middle of the learning process "(Saeful, October, 2017).

IT-based learning with the ipad learning media initiates a learning model called the Creative Problem Solving Process. This model is a flexible tool that can be applied to test real problems and issues. This learning is very potential to train students to be active and creative in dealing with various problems, both personal and group problems to be solved. Learners learn by themselves to identify the causes of problems and alternatives to solve the problem. The teacher's task in this case is to facilitate and direct students, provide a problem for students and look for additional materials that are appropriate with the material by accessing the internet using the ipad.

According to As'ari in Suyitno (2006) learning that is able to train students to think highly is called as problem-based learning. IT-based learning with Ipad Learning is one of the learning models used by teachers in the learning process by utilizing ipad media. This learning can stimulate students to play an active and more independent and more critical role in thinking that starts from looking for data until formulating conclusions so that students can support the meaning from learning activities. In the process of learning ipad, there must be factors that can support and hinder the application of learning. The supporting factors include Ipad is a learning media that has perfect quality so that it can support the learning process, Ipad can adjust to the development of existing computerized technology facilities, IPad can train and familiarize students to be more independent in learning, IPad can stimulate the development of students' thinking progress to solve the problems faced appropriately, Ipad Can make school education more relevant to life and the various features of iPad can certainly support learning in terms of visuals, students become easy to understand and memorize the subject matter quickly.

Apart from that, the inhibiting factors of IT-based learning include the concept of ipad learning cannot be followed by those who do not master or d required facilities, it requires a longer time allocation compared to other learning methods,the concept of ipad learning, especially on this ibook feature is still in the level of development stage, so it still needs improvement in the next stage (Rahardja: 89-90).

4.3 Student learning outcomes after the Implementation of IT-Based Learning with Ipad Learning in the eight grade of Sabilurrasyad Junior High school Bojong shows well improvements

Based on the results of interviews and observations, outcomes of students are also influenced by the learning media used. This includes the implementation of IT-based learning with this Ipad learning, which can be seen from the development of cognitive, affective and social aspects of students in the past learning. If it is known that there is an increase in learning outcomes than before, then the implementation of IT-based Islamic learning through the media of ipad learning is successful. This is in accordance with Khoiriyyah (2017) as a Islamic Religion teacher at Sabilurrasyad Junior High School:

"Student learning outcomes can be seen from their learning behavior, which is seen in terms of cognitive, affective, and psychomotor. In terms of cognitive, for example, students are more critical and independent in responding to a problem or material that they do not know by looking for it using an ipad without always depending on the teacher. In terms of affective, for example, students who are initially not enthusiastic and lack enthusiasm in learning, after the use of learning students are more enthusiastic, more active, and enthusiastic in participating in learning. In terms of psychomotor, it can be seen from the students' expertise in practicing the material taught, because they can absorb the lessons through the material or video that I broadcast "(Khoiriyah, August, 2017).

The following are the observations of the researchers on the results of daily examinations of the eight grade students in Islmaic Religion Education subject in Sabilurrasyad Junior High School Bojong Ngampel Kendal (Documentation, August, 2017).

Table 1. The Score of Islamic Religion Education at the Eighth Graders of Sabilurrasyad Junior High School

Total Recapitulati on	**First Meeting (before using Ipad)**	**Second Meeting (After using Ipad**
Scores	2272	2399
Average	81,14	85,67

It is clearly known that the average value for the eight grade students before being applied to the learning was 81.14. After the learning of Ipad media was applied, the average value of the eight grade students was 85.67. This is in accordance with Febrika (2017):

"The changes that I felt after applying IT-based learning with Ipad Learning were that I was more enthusiastic in following the learning process and also trained me to be active and think creatively in solving problems related to the PAI material provided by the teacher. With these changes, my learning achievements are also increasing "(Febrika, August, 2017).

From the above description, it can be analyzed that the implementation of ipad learning media is inseparable from the existence of supporting and inhibiting factors, especially in technical ways both for the teacher and students. However, the existence of supporting and inhibiting factors in the implementation of this learning will make subject teachers more creative and innovative in creating an atmosphere of learning. In addition, the existence of the above factors will make the teacher more mature in managing learning, paying more attention to his students, making considerations and determining policies so that the learning can run well and enhance better results.

5. Conclusion

The application of IT-based learning through the media of Ipad Learning in Islmaic Religion Education subjects at Sabilurrasyad Junior High school, Bojong Ngampel Kendal can be considered effective. This can be proven by changes in student learning behavior when learning. Students are more motivated by their learning motivation. However, supporting and inhibiting factors for the implementation of class VIII PAI learning with Ipad learning media include the existence of ipad facilities and equipped with internet networks provided by schools, the training of the Central Java Province Information and Communication Technology Development Agency which was attended by teachers so that it could be used as a provision for teachers to implement IT-based learning using ipad, the material was available on iPad, iPad attracts students' attention and motivation, iPad can present audio-visual material and train students to be active and creative by looking for additional material using iPad. On the other hand, the inhibiting factors include iPad is an electronic device so it has limited battery power or usage, unstable internet network, some students cannot use iPad, there is no filter to block sites that are inappropriate for students and somehow students abuse it by accessing sites outside of material.

References

1. Ishak, A. & Darmawan, D. *Technology of Education*, (Bandung, Remaja Rosdakarya, 2015)
2. Ahmad, M. A.Q., *Methodology of Islamic Religion Teaching*, (Jakarta, Rineka Cipta, 2008)
3. Alim, M., *Islamic Religion education; An effort of building Muslim Thinking and Identity*, (Bandung, Remaja RosdaKarya, 2006)
4. Asmani, J., M, *Tips of Effective Information and Communication Technology Utilization in Education*, (Jogjakarta, Diva Press, 2011)
5. Darmawan, D., *Technology of Teaching*, (Bandung, Remaja Rosdakarya, 2012)
6. Depdiknas, *Standard of Islamic Religion Education Competence in Junior High School*, (Jakarta, Depdiknas, 2003)
7. Desrianti, et al, Audio Visual as One The Teaching Resources on ILearning, *Journal of CCIT*. **5**, 2 (2011)
8. Dimyati & Moedjiono, *Teaching and Learning*, (Jakarta: Rineka Cipta, 2009)
9. Febrika, (August, 2017). Interview with Febrika-Student of Sabilurrasyad Junior High School
10. Ghofur, A., (August, 2017). Interview with Ghofur-Headmaster of Sabilurrasyad Junior High School
11. Hadisi, La & Wa Muna, 2015, Management of Information Technology in Creating Inovation Model, *Journal of al-Ta'dib*, **8**, 1,(2015)
12. Henderi, et al., Penggunaan Metode Ilearning Untuk Meningkatkan Kualitas Pembelajaran di Perguruan Tinggi, *Journal of CCIT* (2012)
13. Khoiriyyah, (August, 2017). Interview with Khoiriyyah-Teacher of Sabilurrasyad Junior High School
14. Husain, C., Utilization of Information and Communication Technology at Tarakan Muhammadiyah Senior High Schppl, *Journal of Education Policy and Development*, **2**, 2. (2014)
15. Maswan & Muslimin, 2017, *Education Technology*, (Jogjakarta, Pustaka Pelajar, 2017)
16. Miarso, *Definition of education technology*,(Jakarta, Rajawali, 1986)
17. Rahardja, U. et al, Ibooks Standardisation And Good Practice For Effective Education Methods In Support Of Ilearning, *Journal of CCIT*. **5**, 1 (2011)
18. Saeful, (August, 2017). Interview with Saeful-Student of Sabilurrasyad Junior High School
19. Shoimin, A. , Model of Inovative Learning in 2013 Curriculum, (Yogyakarta, Ar-ruzz Media, 2014)
20. Ula, (August, 2017). Interview with Ula-Student of Sabilurrasyad Junior High School

Development of Open Journal System 3.0

Yoris Adi Maretta*, *Totok* Sumaryanto, *Yuli* Utanto, *Kustiono* Kustiono, and *Sri Maryati* Deliana

Universitas Negeri Semarang, Indonesia

Abstract. This study aims to develop an Open Journal System 3.0 and test the effectiveness of the open journal system 3.0 as a media student learning resources. This research method using research procedures Research and Development. The results showed acquire material expert assessment of the percentage of 94.44% while the assessment of media experts journals obtain a percentage of 97.77%. The results of testing the effectiveness of t count> t table (20 945> 2.000) and significance <0.05 (0.000 <0.05), then Ho is rejected. So we can conclude there are differences in the effectiveness of this research on the development of open journal 3.0 system that is used as a medium for student learning resources. This may imply that the development of open journal 3.0 system influence on student effectiveness in finding learning resources and the ease of downloading the article.

1 Introduction

Website E-Journal lecturers and students using the platform Open Journal System 3.0. Open Journal System 3.0 is a management platform of scientific journals online. OJS 3 enables journal managers to migrate from offline to online management system. Starting from a manuscript / article posted by the author, the process of reviewing, tracking, and so forth until the manuscript is accepted for publication in a journal, everything can be done with OJS 3 [1]. According Willinsky (2005) with this system the process of sending manuscripts / articles (submission), assessment, editing, layout editing and publishing can be done online. OJS 3 itself was developed by the Public Knowledge Project (PKP). Public Knowledge Project is an organization founded in 1998 by John Willinsky University of British Columbia. Since then PKP has grown and evolved into a virtual operation with two international and institutional anchor at Stanford University and Simon Fraser University Library [2].

OJS 3 is a web-based information system, so it requires Apache web server and recommended using a server-based, such as debian, ubuntu, redhat, Suse and other OS servers [3]. Comparison with the media website management journals such as wordpress, jomla, Moodle, the OS server on OJS 3-based This has the advantage especially of better security, faster access, lightweight system and also the software that is free and freely developed by anyone [4]

Unnes problems faced during this time was to see Open Journal System 3.0 is fairly standard and rigid, making the reader / user difficult to operate. During this time the reader is hard to find the desired article in the online journal. Whether it's the students and faculty. In addition to these problems, the difficulty in accessing the posting, journal editors list, see the visitor counter is not clearly visible because the view is still the standard. Not only that issue, see the layout of the article also does not meet the national standard layout journal articles. There are still some weaknesses, such as web E-Journal, volume, issue, the issue of the journal, correspondence address, date received, approved and published and issued by whom also lacking [5].

2 Methods

This research method using research procedures Research and Development. Research and Development can be defined as the research methods used to produce a specific product and test the effectiveness of these products [6]

Before doing the development, the first data collection. In this phase, three ways of collecting data that is observation, interviews and questionnaires. Observation is a method of collecting data using observations of the research object [5]. Data collection techniques such as observation and interviews intended to seek potential and problems that have been experienced by visitors of the students in the sample. Observations and interviews were conducted by visiting the Office Developer Library Journal Unnes Building G Floor 1 Campus Unnes sekaran Gunungpati [7].

3 Results and Discussion

Samples are partly or representative of the population studied. The use of the test was given to 51 students a sample of the population of students from the Department of Education Technology totaling 334 students. Consisting of 15% 1,3,5,7 semester students. The population is the totality of all possible values, the results of counting or measurement, quantitative and qualitative data about the particular characteristics of all members of a collection of complete and clear we want to learn its properties [8]

A number of written questions questionnaire was used to obtain information from respondents in terms of his personal report, or the things he knew. In the test phase of use, provides research to a sample questionnaire to distinguish the old look of the website and the new (after development). Samples were asked to analyze the website to see the old and the new after development.

This test aims to prove the significance of the difference between before and after product development. Therefore, it needs to be tested statistically by t-test correlated (related). Analysis of data from the development of open journal system 3.0 with t-test, which is to test the hypothesis as follows:

Ho: There is no difference in the effectiveness of the search for learning resources by the use of e-journal before development.

Ha: There is no difference in the effectiveness of the search for learning resources by the use of e-journal after development

Analysis of the observed data before and after development with the help of SPSS application, the application used for data processing. Based on the output table Paired Samples Statistics can be seen that in the table are average values obtained from the experimental first stage is 13.31 with a standard deviation obtained at 1.225 and standard error of the mean 171. While the second stage of the experimental results obtained by the average 15.98 with a standard deviation of 1.334 and standard error of the mean 187. the values were obtained from 51 respondents who entered the data.

Based on the output table Paired Samples Correlations obtained correlation value of 0.751 with 0.000 significance (below 0.05). This means on a new design that is after the development of the open journal system 3.0 has contributed a total of 0,751 of the old design, where the e-journal is not in the design and prior to the development.

Paired Samples T Test was used to determine whether there are differences in effectiveness between before and after the development of open journal system 3.0. Tests using two-sided tests with significance level $\alpha = 5\%$ level of significance in this case means taking the risk of wrong in taking the decision to reject the hypothesis that right as much as 5% (5% significance or 0:05 is the standard measure often used in research. from the table above were obtained t value is 20.945 and 0.000 significance (below 0.05).

To determine the value of t table can be seen in the statistics table on the 0.05: 2 = 0.025 (two-tailed test) with degrees of freedom (df) n-1 or 51-1 = 50.

According to the table above Paired Samples Test note that the value t count> t table (20 945> 2.000) and significance <0.05 (0.000 <0.05), then Ho is rejected. Thus, we can conclude that there are differences in the effectiveness of the development of open journal system 3.0 that is used as a medium of learning resources students. This may imply that the development of open journal system 3.0 that is on the website www.journal.unnes.ac.id/sju an impact on the effectiveness of students in finding the source of learning and ease of downloading articles [5].

4 Conclusion

Based on the analysis of research data obtained by value t count> t table (20 945> 2.00) and significance <0.05 (0.000 <0.05), then Ho is rejected. Thus, it can be concluded that the development is done by a very effective to be used as a medium of learning resources students. The ease in accessing e-journal give pleasure in finding the source of learning in e-journal website Unnes. Development is done in the header, see three columns and additional information on the sidebar.

References

1 H. Sotudeh, A. Horri, "Countries positioning in open access journals system: An investigation of citation distribution patterns," *Scientometrics*, **81**, 1, 7–31, (2009).

2 J. Willinsky, "Open Journal Systems," *Libr. Hi Tech*, **23**, 4, 504–519, (2005).

3 B. D. Edgar and J. Willinsky, "A survey of the scholarly journals using Open Journal Systems. Scholarly and Research Communication [Електронний ресурс]," *Режим доступу*, **1**, 1, 1–5, (2005).

4 Y. A. Maretta; A. Munib; S. Sukirman, "Pengembangan Open Journal System Sebagai Sumber Belajar Mahasiswa," *Innov. J. Curric. Educ. Technol.*, **3**, 1, (2016).

5 R. Bogdan and S. Biklen, "Qualitative research for education: An introduction to theory and practice." Boston: Allyn and Bacon, (2007).

6 T. Sumaryanto, *Metodologi Penelitian 2*. Semarang: Universitas Negeri Semarang, (2010).

7 Y. Utanto, G. P. Widhanarto, and Y. A. Maretta, "A web-based portfolio model as the students' final assignment: Dealing with the development of higher education trend," in *AIP Conference Proceedings*, 1818, 1, 20063 (2017).

8 P. H. Rossi, M. W. Lipsey, and H. E. Freeman, *Evaluation: A systematic approach*. Sage publications, (2003).

Effectiveness study on applied quality assurance of ducational technology in learning quality improvement in universities

Haryono[*], *Titi* Prihatin, *Ghanis Putra* Widhanarto

Universitas Negeri Semarang, Indonesia

Abstract. Educational technology is an applied scientific discipline that develops by the need of the field , namely the demands of learning more effectively, efficiently, broadly, widely, and quickly. As a systematic and systematic process in helping to solve learning problems, the application of educational technology can be directed to the learning quality assurance process. This study is aimed at: (1) analyzing the application of educational technology in improving the quality of learning in universities, (2) analyzing the quality assurance process of learning in universities, and (3) testing the effectiveness of quality assurance models based on applied educational technology in improving the quality of learning in College. The method used is a quantitative approach. The study began with an exploratory survey method, then continued with experiments. The results showed that the analysis of the quality of learning in universities was very dependent on the application of educational technology, the learning quality assurance process agreed that educational technology could improve the quality of learning in universities, and the application of quality assurance models based on applied learning technology is effective to improve the quality of learning in college high. The benefits of this study as a reference for the development model of quality assurance, especially for education and learning.

1 Introduction

Learning activity is the main of the educational process that takes place within each educational unit or institution. Professional educators are responsible for achieving quality learning through the creation of meaningful learning experiences for students, in addition for facilitating students to gain the maximum learning outcomes. Schools or education units are responsible for building a quality learning system so that they are able to contribute fully to the intellectual development, attitudes and morals of students in a complete harmonization (Haryono, 2016).

The quality of learning is needed to make an education that can create students in better learning capacity. Quality learning will lead students not only to acquire a number of knowledge, skills and attitudes, but more important is to develop their learning capacity on how to acquire knowledge, skills and attitude (Zamroni, 2000; Semiawan, 1998). Therefore the quality of learning is needed as a criterion dimension to be a benchmark for professional development of educators as well as the development of schools as educational institutions that must consistently develop towards competition in the information and openness era of the world.

Related to efforts to improve the quality of learning that must be sought by every professional educator, educational technology is present to provide enlightenment. Educational technology as an area of interest with an effort to facilitate the learning process with characteristics; (1) provide special attention and unique services from each of the target students, (2) use variety and as many learning resources as possible, and (3) apply a systems approach (Miarso, 2002). Educational technology is not just an application of technology products in education, but is a systematic and systemic process to enable a higher quality education and learning process. Although it is undeniable that in the system process it allows for the application of technology in the meaning of the product (Haryono, 2008).

Applied educational technology in the learning system, has the potential to improve the quality of learning that has an impact on the acquisition of student learning outcomes. Praxis of learning cannot be separated from the application of educational technology. Quality learning can only be realized, when properly designed, equipped with the necessary materials, presented through the media and the use of appropriate resources, the division of roles is clearly defined based on function, and properly assessed (Haryono, 2008). This prerequisite is a field of educational technology work both theoretically and practically.

Applied education technology functionally can be directed to the learning quality assurance process. Educational technology that is conceptually defined as study and ethical practice in facilitating learning and improving performance through the creation, utilization and management of appropriate technological processes and resources (Januszewski & Molenda, 2008). The quality assurance process can be developed by basing and applying the basic principles of educational technology. Quality assurance of educational technology-based learning can be directed at efforts; (1) building a culture of quality among the components of the learning system in schools, (2) the division of tasks and responsibilities that are clear and proportional among the components of the learning system in schools, (3) the internal school setting starts about the quality standards of learning that are committed of all components in the learning system, and (4) the establishment of a learning quality information system in the education unit. Quality assurance of learning is developed with the principles of sustainable, planned and systematic with a clear and measurable time frame and quality achievement targets, respecting school autonomy, facilitating the achievement of quality learning, and improving the quality of education in a sustainable manner (Haryono, 2016).

2 Methods

Referring to the objectives to be achieved, this research program was designed with a quantitative approach with quasi-experimental and survey methods. The survey was conducted to examine the application of educational technology in improving the quality of learning and the quality assurance process of learning in universities, while the quasi-experimental method with pretest posttest control group design was conducted to test the effectiveness of educational technology-based quality assurance in improving the quality of learning. Technically the research method that will be conducted to answer research questions can be explained as follows.

In accordance with the objectives of the study and the characteristics of the data collected, the analysis is carried out descriptively and inferentially. Descriptive analysis was carried out to see trends in relation to the variables under study, while inferential analysis was carried out to test hypotheses regarding the effectiveness-based quality assurance of educational technologyin improving the quality of learning in universities.

3 Results

The applied model of quality assurance learning system in comprehensive education technology can be visualized in the flow chart as follows.

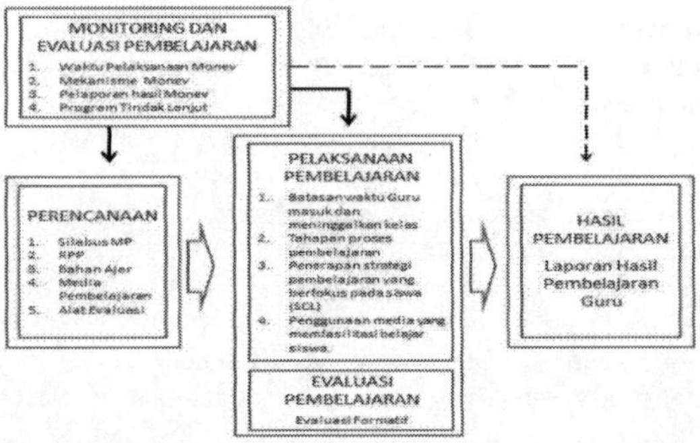

Fig 1. Quality Assurance Model for Applied Based LearningTechnology Education

The quality assurance model of education technology based learning as a process of monitoring and evaluating learning is carried out through three stages, namely learning planning, implementation of learning processes, monitoring and evaluation of learning. In the learning planning stage, the process of preparing Semester Learning Plans (RPS), developing instructional materials, developing learning media, and measuring learning outcomes by lecturers is developed. The validation process of learning planning by the lecturer is done to get results in accordance with the established quality assurance standards.

The quality assurance stage is then carried out in the learning process. The implementation of learning quality assurance is carried out during the learning process where the quality assurance team validates whether the learning is carried out in accordance with the planning that was made in the previous stage. Furthermore, the monitoring and evaluation of the implementation of learning activities is carried out as the third or final stage in the quality assurance of learning based on applied educational technology.

Monitoring and evaluation is carried out by periodic monitoring and evaluation, namely the beginning of the semester, mid-semester, and the end of the semester. The results of monitoring and evaluation are then reported periodically in accordance with the monitoring and evaluation activities carried out. The results of the monitoring and evaluation were held by the stakeholders to conduct follow-up programs as an effort to improve the quality of learning quality, as well as a material of self-reflection for the improvement of further learning.

3.1 Applied Educational Technology in Improving the Quality of Learning in Higher Education

Revealing the application of educational technology in higher education there are results that state that there is still a lack of applied quality assurance models in learning. From the data taken shows the results that educational technology is applied to certain fields, namely:

1. Lecturer Competence in the Application of Educational Technology proven by teaching experience of less than 10 years stated that in higher education implemented educational technology but only a few respondents.
2. Implementation of Educational Technology in Praxis Learning shows very good results, the average lecturer with teaching experience under 10 years has implemented educational technology in the praxis of learning.
3. Impact of Application of Educational Technology in Achieving Learning Quality in Universities from research results stated that the high use of learning media, teaching materials, learning-specific services, electronic learning resources, and systems approaches to learning have been carried out but have not yet reached all parties.

3.2 Quality Assurance Process of Learning in Higher Education

Learning standards include, planning, implementing, monitoring and evaluating learning. There is evidence

found that the standard of learning has been done very well.
The learning quality assurance mechanism starts with monitoring, the distribution of courses, RPS endorsement, and monev have been done well but only mostly.
Learning quality assurance instruments and instruments are proven by quality assurance response questionnaires, learning quality assurance standards, operational standards for developing instructional materials, operational standards for learning media development procedures, quality assessment matrices for learning in universities. So it was concluded that all parties had done it.

3.3 The Effectiveness of Applied Quality Assurance Models Educational Technology in Improving the Quality of Learning in Higher Education

1. appropriateness of the learning process standards is proven by the Lecturers validating the devices that contain preliminary activities, core activities and closing activities, the ability of the lecturer to speak (tone, intonation, expression) well, and able to listen, the ability of the lecturer to explain something abstract into something that is easy to understand, the ability of lecturers related to the visualization of ideas in the form of communicative presentation materials through various media and relevant technology tools. So that the learning process standard has been implemented very well.
2. Its usefulness for the development of quality culture in universities has increased the interaction of lecturers and students using technology, there has been an increase in the number of electronic teaching materials used in lectures, there has been an increase in the availability of technology support facilities provided by the campus. and the relevance of the material presented by the lecturer with the development of scientific discipline, and being able to take advantage of the results of related research.

4 Discussion

Learning is a systematic and deliberate effort to create educational interaction between students and learning resources, so that learning occurs in students. Learning is a deliberate effort, purposeful, controlled so that other people learn or occur changes that are relatively settled (Miarso, 2004).
Applied educational technology in the teaching and learning process at several universities in Central Java shows that good academic interaction has occurred. hasyim wahid university runs the application of educational technology Educational
technology as an applied discipline, developing by the need in the field, namely the need to learn more effectively, efficiently, widely, quickly, and so on. For that there is a product that is intentionally developed for the sake of learning, and there is something that is found and can be utilized for the same benefit. Educational technology is a systemic process in helping to solve human learning problems throughout life, anywhere, anytime, by any means, and by anyone (Miarso, 2004).
Furthermore, referring to the definition of *technology education is the study and ethical practice of facilitating and improving performance by creating, using, and managing appropriate technological processes and resources* (Januszewski & Molenda, 2008), educational technology can contribute theoretically and practically in improving the quality of learning.
Quality assurance of learning in universities is a strategic step in realizing standardized learning services and continuous quality improvement efforts. The learning quality assurance system is based on applied educational technology, based on the results of Haryono's research (2015-2016), in which it contains; (1) limitations and scope of quality assurance of learning in universities, (2) quality and organizational policies, (3) quality standards of learning and mechanisms for achievement, (4) manuals for quality learning and instruments.

Conclusion

The results showed that the analysis of the quality of learning in college depends on the application of educational technology, the learning quality assurance process agreed that educational technology can improve the quality of learning in universities, and the application of quality assurance models based on applied learning technology is effective to improve the quality of learning in College.

References

1. Haryono. 2008. "Applied Errors in Educational Technology in Praxis of Forgotten Learning". Speech inauguration of Professor of Unnes Education Technology. Semarang, February 26, 2008. Downloaded June 2017 from http://blog.unnes.ac.id/fransharyono.
2. Haryono, et al. 2016. "Implementation of Quality Assurance Based on Applied Educational Technology". Research Report (Unpublished). LP2M Unnes.
3. Januszewski, Alan and Michael Molenda. 2008. Educational Technology: A Definition with Commentary. New York: Taylor & Francis Group.
4. Miarso, Yusufhadi. 2002. "Concepts and Applied Learning Technology", Paper in the First Lecture of TP S2 UNNES Students, September 14, 2002.
5. Semiawan, Conny R. 1998. Higher Education: Improving Human Ability as Optimum as possible. Jakarta: Directorate General of Higher Education Ministry of Education and Culture.
6. Zamroni. 2000. Educational Paradigm of the Future. Yogyakarta: Bigraf Publishing.

LPTK contribution in development of sustainable teachers professionalism in semarang district

*Sukirman**, *Yuli* Utanto, *Yoris Adi* Maretta

Universitas Negeri Semarang, Indonesia

Abstract. This study aims to portray the condition of teachers' competencies and problems as well as the ongoing implementation of teacher professional development in Semarang district, Central Java. Based on the problem mapping found, the solution was obtained by involving the Education Institution of Education Personnel. This study used a survey approach in Semarang District which was carried out throughout 2016. Data collection was done by giving open questions to respondents and followed up with in-depth interviews. Respondents consisted of teachers, principals, and school supervisors. The results of the study showed that, in terms of the shortage of Civil Servant class teachers, the role of non Civil Servant class teachers was very large, namely 17% of the total class teacher needs. It means that if there is no non Civil Servant class teacher available then 17% of the study group does not get optimal learning services. 130 public elementary schools have a ratio of <= 16 students per study group. In those small schools the required class teachers are 757 teachers, the Civil Servant teachers available are 563 teachers. Those schools require 194 more teachers, meanwhile the non-Civil Servant teachers available are only 165 teachers. The other findings have not been analysed for its training needs, the performance evaluations have not been objective, there is some difficulty in finding the training funds and resource persons, the training activities are still sporadic, and monitoring and evaluation have not been done. It is recommended to do regrouping especially to be focused on the small schools. Small school is a school with a ratio of <= 16 students per study group. Implementing multigrade learning models in small schools is necessary because doing regrouping is not possible due to the geographical conditions. It is also necessary for the District Education Office and the Education Institution of Education Personnel to establish close cooperation, the lecturers can be consultants in the district, and the implementation of ongoing teacher professional development is carried out seriously in accordance with established guidelines and regulations.

1 Introduction

Professional teachers are a certainty. Demands in professional teachers have been stated clearly in the regulation number 20 year 2003 concerning the National Education System, the regulation number 14 of 2005 concerning Teachers and Lecturers, and Government Regulation Number 74 of 2008 concerning Teachers. Professional teachers are required to meet academic qualifications of at least S1 (bachelor degree) / D4 (diploma 4) and have a certificate as an educators. In order to acquire an educator certificate, a teacher must meet the four competencies namely; professional competence, pedagogic competence, social competence, and personality competence.

In fact, there are still many Indonesian teacher who haven't met professional standard yet. This can be seen from the number of teachers who have not fulfilled the academic qualifications of S1 (bachelor degree) / D4 (Diploma 4) and have no certificate of educator yet. The Ministry of Education and Culture data in 2012 shows that 49% of teachers have not had an S1 / D4 education. Meanwhile 40% of teachers do not have the certificate of educator. The worse case, many of the teachers who already have the certificate of educator are showing lack of competence. The government is targeting that the certified teachers to get a teacher competency test (UKG) score of at least 70, but in fact 2012 teacher data in Indonesia showing the average value of 45 from the required 70 (Baswedan, 2014). Seeing this fact, the government continues to improve the competency standard of educators to 80 with the hope that teachers will be more motivated to increase their competence and professionalism.

Teachers who are actively teaching on schools must be improved professionally on an ongoing basis. For this reason the Ministry of Education and Culture created a program called Continuing Professional Development (PKB) for the active teachers. According to the Ministry of State Secretary and Bureaucratic Reform No. 16 of 2009 concerning the Teacher's Functional Position and Credit Score, PKB is the development of teacher competencies that are carried out in accordance with the needs, gradually, continuously to improve teacher professionalism.

According to Seyfarth (2002), PKB is an opportunity given to teachers, other professionals, and support personnel to gain new knowledge and attitudes, therefore it will maintain behavioral change so as to improve student achievement. This activity is a process to maintain and improve the skills, attitudes, understanding, or performance of professional teachers. Unfortunately, based on the results of Nurkolis and Yovitha's (2015) research in three districts in Central Java, PKB has not

* Corresponding author: sukirmantp@mail.unnes.ac.id

been effective. The implementation of PKB starts at the school, group, and district levels is not yet running effectively. 63% of PKB implementation at various stages of activities ranging from planning to implementation has not been ran effectively.
Based on the above conditions, it is important to involve the Education Institute for Education Personnel (LPTK) as a center for sustainable professional development for teachers. If the current LPTKs policy is the pre-service training, then the portion of in-service training services must be improved. Especially the fact that the teachers who have been graduated from the LPTK in the previous year are showing lack of performance.

2 Method

This survey research was conducted in Semarang District, Central Java throughout 2016. Data analysis was based on respondents' answers to open questions given via e-mail followed by in-depth interviews. Questionnaires were sent to around 300 teachers, principals, and school supervisors during this period and only 1.1% of respondents answered according to expectations. Based on information from the respondents, researchers conducted in-depth interviews with them to follow up on the written answers they had previously sent.

3 Discussion

Semarang Regency wich has a total of 531 primary schools and 92 junior high schools along with the geographical conditions of having mountains and valleys certainly has faced many problems concerning the arrangement and equity of teachers and the professional development of teachers in a sustainable manner. Based on the data analysis in the field, researcher is able to map out the urgent issues to find solutions immediately, including:
First; Classroom Teacher Problems. The number of public primary schools whose data can be processed is 495 schools with 3019 study groups, meaning that in public elementary schools, 3019 classroom teachers are needed. Semarang District has only 2466 Civil Servant class teacher, so there are still 553 Civil Servant class teachers needed. On the other hand there are 524 non Civil Servant classroom teachers available, so the study groups that have not been taken by Civil Servant classroom teachers would be handled by the Non-Civil Servant classroom teachers and principals. Judging from the shortage of Civil Servant classroom teachers availability, the role of non Civil Servant class teachers is very important, namely fulfilling the 17% of the total classroom teachers needed. This means that if there is no Non-Civil Servant class teachers available, then 17% of the study group does not get an optimal learning services. Not to mention the class teachers who will be retired within the next 5 years are 364 people. The distribution of Non-Civil Servant class teachers is also uneven, in 10 sub-districts the number of Non-Civil Servant class teachers exceeds the needs, while the other 9 sub-districts lack of Non-Civil Servant classroom teachers.
Second; Teachers of Islam Religion Education (PAI) in Elementary School. The need of PAI teachers in Public Elementary Schools is 377 teachers, while there are only 302 Civil Servant of PAI teachers available, so it needs 75 teachers more. Meanwhile, there are still 118 non Civil Servant PAI teachers available, so there are 43 PAI teachers surplus. The surplus will not be a problem because there are a lot of teachers who will be retired soon. Within the next 5 years, there will be 143 PAI teachers will be retired. So the excess of 43 PAI teachers will later become a shortage of teachers. For the Physical Education subject, the teachers needed are 440 teachers, while there are only 313 Civil Servant teachers available. So, there are 127 teachers needed. For this case, there are 93 non Civil Servant teachers available, so the total shortage of teachers is only 34 people, while teachers who will retire within the next 5 years are 7 people.
Third; Small schools in Elementary School level of Semarang district are quite a problem. 130 public elementary schools have a ratio of <= 16 students per study group. In these small schools the need for class teachers is 757 teachers, the Civil Servant classroom teachers available are 563 teachers, it needs 194 teachers more, while non-Civil Servant teachers available are only 165 teachers. For the teachers' qualifications, some Civil Servant teachers in public elementary schools haven't had S1 / D4 degree, they are 39% of the classroom teachers, 48% of the PAI teachers are still 48%, and 35% of physical education teachers. Some of them are in process of completing the S1 / DIV study, while the others are approaching retirement period, so they decided to not continue their studies for S1 / DIV degree.
Fourth; Teacher certification, 35% of total Civil Servant classroom teachers in public elementary schools have not been certified, they are 16% of PAI teachers, and 46% of physical education teachers. Some teachers who have not been certified are still in the process of taking PLPG, a sstudy for teachers to get professional education certificate. In addition, teachers who will enter retirement age, based on DAPODIK data for the next 5 years, they are 364 teachers or 15%. While in the next 10 years they will be 1113 teachers or 45%. For PAI teachers, the next 5 years will be 142 teachers or 38% teachers retired, and for the next 10 years there will be 259 teachers or 69%. For physical education teachers, in the next 5 years there will be 7 people or 2% teachers, and in the next 10 years will be 106 teachers or 24% teachers will be retired. The high percentage of teachers who will enter retirement within the next 5-10 years must be anticipated with accurate teacher needs planning so that the problem of lacking so many teacher will not be occured, and the learning process in class can be guaranteed.
Fifth; Arrangement and Equity of Teachers in Junior High Schools. Based on the results of the teachers need calculation for schools aggregated at the district level for 10 subjects in Junior High School, the need for subject teachers are 1178 teachers, while the Civil Servant teachers are only 1027 teachers, so it needs 152 Civil

Servant teachers more. On the other hand, there are 146 non-Civil Servant subject teachers available, so in total it needs 6 non-Civil Servant subject teachers. Teachers of Science, Social Sciences, and PKN are overstaffed of 7 teachers while the other subjects are lacked of teachers. The junior high school teachers calculation using teacher mobility model resulting the needs of 1028 Civil Servant teachers, while the number of Civil Servant teachers available are 1026 teachers, so it lacks of 2 teachers. On the other hand, there are 146 non-Civil Servant teachers available, so the total surplus of non-Civil Servant teachers is 144 teachers. Subjects which are still lacking of teachers are English, Mathematics, Islamic Education, Physical Education, ICT, but the needs is less than before. The other four subjects' teachers are surplus while cultural arts subject lacks / excess of 0 teachers.

Sixth; Based on the calculation result of the teacher's needs, it seems that all this time the calculation of teacher needs is calculated per school, the shortage of Civil Servant teachers in schools is immediately overcome by certifying non Civil Servant into civil servant teachers. The problem occured when the teacher's needs are calculated with the mobility mode. In 4 subjects, the teachers are overloaded while in the other 5 subjects there is a shortage of teachers. In total, the excess of non Civil Servant subject teachers are 144 teachers. The alternative policy chosen is the mobilization of Civil Servant subject teachers in a coordinated way and controlling the certification of the non Civil Servant teacher. The education office must map the teaching duty of teachers for those who have not fulfilled the obligation to teach for 24 hours. The education office must also has a map of the need for subject teachers per school, so that they can give an alternative solution for teachers who have not been able to fulfill the 24 hours teaching obligation.

Seventh, the use of information and communication technology (ICT) among teachers in Semarang District is still relatively low. This is based on the small number of respondents who answered via email; only 1.1% of them. This is a fact that teachers, school principals, and school supervisors are not used to using e-mail to support their work as educators. After being interviewed deeper, it was proven that those who had the email address claimed they had not used it regularly in supporting their professional duties. They rarely open the email, even to be used as a means of sharing information with fellow educators. A teacher even admitted that he only opened his e-mail only every 6 months and having an e-mail is only to make sure that he can provide it in case a fellow teacher or the principal asked for it.

This finding contrasts with the habits of professional educators in developed countries who always use email to support the learning process. Even in developed countries they used to using e-mail and opening websites to send and receive assignments that have been done by their students. Educators in developed countries are accustomed to browse learning resources online, including searching for research results in current research journals. Reports from the National Center for Education Statistic (2009) state that, in developed countries when surveying the use of ICT in schools, 80% -81% of the teachers respond to the online surveys.

In such conditions, the LPTK which has many ICT experts can become partners of the Semarang District Education Office to provide ICT training in learning process to the teachers. ICT knowledge and skills in education are indispensable, given the rapid development of science, knowledge, technology and art.

Eighth, analysis of the need of teachers training is not yet available. Related to the implementation of PKB at the district, cluster and school level, the dominant problem is the absence of intensive socialization from the Semarang District Education Office. In fact, respondents claimed that they did not know whether the PKB implementation team had been established or not. The teacher also does not understand whether there is a budget allocated from the regional budget and income (ABPD) or other sources to fund the implementation of the PKB. Because of the lack of socialization, as a result many teachers were not aware of the PKB program. Respondents claimed that they rarely received training held by the Semarang District Education Office. Even the news was heard among teachers and principals, the selection of people to be sent to a training had not been well planned, but was based on closeness with officials in the District Education Office. When this complaint was confirmed to the Semarang District Education Office, their answers were astonishing, because they claimed they did not have the training maps needed by the teachers, who needed what training, and at what level the training for teachers was needed. This means that the Semarang District Education Office does not yet have a map and training need assessment for teachers in their area.

LPTKs especially those with Curriculum and Technology Education study programs need to intervene to help Semarang District Education Office to provide training on the required training analysis. This analysis starts from mapping the teacher's abilities and is continued with the type and level of training needed by the teacher to improve his competence. Helping hands from the LPTK can undoubtedly spur an increase in teacher professional development competencies.

Third, the teacher performance assessment (PKG) which is the basis for implementing the PKB program has not been done objectively. During the past year, the Semarang District Education Office tried to assess teacher performance. The teacher performance appraisal process is handed over to school principals and senior teachers in each education unit. In fact, the process of assessing teachers in schools has not gone well as it should. According to the acknowledgment of senior teachers and principals, due to their closeness and humanity they cannot bear the need to give a bad assessment to the teacher that they value, even though in reality it is bad because it concerns the development of one's career. They claimed that they assess the teacher not based on reality, but rather used consideration of feelings of compassion. As a result, the assessment given to the 100% majority teacher showed very good results.

The lack of objectivity of the principal and senior teacher's assessment is not without reason. Respondents

stated that it was a demand from the District Education Office, because there has been a rumored message around which states to not to give a teacher bad assessment because this also concerns the good name of the District Education Office. In fact, unfortunately, if there is a senior teacher or headmaster who gives an assessment based on the conditions as real as that which is bad, he is considered not able to judge. The existence of this message makes the assessors run the assessment process as a mere formality. And the team of district level assessors did not correct the results of the PKG assessment which the majority showed very good results.
Relevant to the findings of USAID Priority in Central Java Province in 3 districts, namely Batang, Banjarnegara, and Purbalingga. More than 87% of PKG results show very good results. In fact, the PKG results are in contrast to the results of the teacher competency test (UKG) from the same district which shows that more than 85% of teacher competencies in the 3 districts are low. This is proof that PKG that have been carried out during the past year has not functioned properly because the element of subjectivity is high. In general, low teacher competencies will also produce low teacher performance, and conversely high competencies undoubtedly produce good performance.

This finding is to be urgently responded by the LPTK to immediately support and to provide training to senior teachers, principals, school supervisors, and district assessor teams regarding the method and procedures for assessing teacher performance which are proper, correct, measurable and accountable for the results. Indeed, teacher performance appraisal must be carried out using honest, objective, fair, transparent, valid and accountable principles. Teacher performance appraisal must also bring benefits to teachers who are assessed for their performance, namely to improve themselves independently and structurally in order to further improve performance skills.

Fourth, the District Education Office of Semarang has difficulty in obtaining competent human resources for the implementation of PKB. PKB implementation at the district, groups, and school levels turns out to be a problem with the lack of resource persons to provide various kinds of competency improvement training needed. The District Education Office felt that it does not have enough competent human resources to provide training to improve class teacher competencies, subject teachers, curriculum development and learning technology in schools. Whenever a training is carried out, it is often experienced by lack of experts who should be encouraging and motivating teachers to continue improving their professionalism.

The LPTK is the power house of people who are competent in their fields, has sufficient human resources who are experts in the fields of study, methodology, curriculum development and learning technology. It should be necessary to establish mutually beneficial cooperation between the LPTK and the Semarang District Education Office in order to provide training to teachers, principals and supervisors as a real effort to improve teacher professionalism. The cooperation in question can be bound through a memorandum of mutual agreement or a cooperation agreement through a mechanism of memorandum of understanding (MoU) and a memorandum of agreement (MoA).

Ideally, LPTK that has the responsibility of the *Tri Dharma Perguruan Tinggi* have a collaboration scheme with the Semarang District Education Office through a research program and community service. As an academic person, every lecturer has a moral responsibility to intervene the improvement of the education condition, so that it is required to conduct research and community service in order to improvethe lecturer career. If the needs of the District Education Office to improve the competence of teachers, principals, and school supervisors can be met in accordance with the needs of lecturers to develop their careers, then there will be a mutual beneficial synergies. This collaboration can be initiated by Study Programs, Faculties, Research and Community Service Institutions or through the Educator's Professional Development Institute at the LPTK.

Fifth, the Semarang District Education Office has difficulties in funding for training in the framework of the PKB. According to the Ministry of Finance analysis, all Regencies and Cities in Central Java Province have a low fiscal capacity. The impact is that district and city governments have difficulty in funding development programs in their regions. Including the difficulty to fund education quality improvement programs. The finance of Semarang Regency also depends heavily on state revenues and transfers from the central government in the form of the General Allocation Fund (DAU) every year.

APBD data for Semarang Regency, an average of 42% of district expenditure for education. Of the total education expenditure, an average of 84% is for salaries of employees both educators and education personnel. Workers who dominate in the education sector are educators or teachers, so in Semarang District as much as 73% of the education budget is allocated for educator salaries and 11% for non-educator salaries. Previously the World Bank study (2009) showed that in almost all districts in Indonesia the education budget reached an average of 28% of the APBD and included expenditure on employee salaries. If employee expenditure is not counted, then the average education budget is only 6% of the APBD. This study shows that, in fact education spending on salaries continues to experience an increase, especially after the payment of teacher professional allowances began in 2007/2008.

This trend is not different from other developing countries, where the majority of education spending is only for salary expenditure. Even in some developing countries, employee salaries can reach 90%. Whereas in developed countries whose management of education is already good, spending on employee salaries is a maximum of 50% -60% (Hendarsjah, 2009). The amount of the education budget which is only for salary expenditure reduces the opportunity to improve the quality of education, especially to develop sustainable teacher professionalism. This is what has been experienced by the Education Office, especially the Semarang Regency during this time, it is difficult to organize training for teachers, principals, and school supervisors in order to improve their competence. After deducting capital expenditure or physical expenditure and routine operational expenditures, the remaining operational budget for improving the competence of educators and education personnel is very limited.

This reality must be responded by the LPTK especially those who have a Curriculum and Learning Technology study program by providing consulting assistance to the Semarang District Education Office to prepare a fair, effective and efficient education budget. LPTKs must make Semarang District Education Office officials aware that the amount of the education budget that is only for teacher salaries will not have a direct impact on improving the quality of education. Also LPTK should consult with the Semarang District Education Office to allocate more education budgets for various trainings in order to improve the competence of educators and education personnel which of course undoubtedly had a direct impact on the quality of education in Semarang Regency.

Sixth, PKB as a vehicle to improve teacher competence has not been programmed and has not been directed properly. Semarang District Education Office, cluster in the form of Teacher Working Groups (KKG) and Subject Teacher Meetings (MGMP), as well as education unit levels have not systematically arranged PKB planning. This is evidenced by the absence of a PKB implementation planning document in each field. An activity program without good planning and implementation is impossible to get good results. PKB that has been carried out so far is still sporadic based on the remaining budget in the current year. So often training programs for teachers, principals, and school supervisors are carried out at the end of the fiscal year after being included in the change budget. Often, teacher training is only used as a means to spend the budget and increase the uptake capacity towards the end of the year if the absorption of the Semarang Regency Government is not as significant as expected.

If PKB continues to be implemented with a scheme like this, any training for teachers will never have a positive impact on improving teacher competence or improving the quality of education in general because it is only project-based. Therefore, systematically planning PKB becomes very important because in fact only 5% of teachers have the opportunity to follow institutionalized professional development. In fact, if the opportunity is given evenly to each teacher, then a teacher has the opportunity to participate in professional development training only once in 20 years (Danim, 2011). In this case the LPTK has a strategic role to train and provide consultation to the Semarang District Education Office to make training plans well and directed, so as to be able to have a positive impact on improving teacher competency in Semarang Regency.

Seventh, other findings in the implementation of PKB both at the district, cluster and school level have never been carried out by monitoring and evaluation to assess the success of PKB programs. About one year the PKB is implemented by the government, never before has there been monitoring and evaluation to assess the implementation of the PKB program. A study has not been conducted to determine the success rate of implementing PKB for teachers to improve their competence or not. LPTK has many of expert human resources who are able to carry out independent and independent monitoring and evaluation. Supposedly, evaluation expert lecturers from the LPTK should provide assistance to the Semarang District Education Office in monitoring and evaluating the implementation of PKB so far. The results of this monitoring and evaluation can be used as a basis for determining steps to improve PKB implementation, analyzing training needs, and designing ideal CLA programs for teachers to improve the quality of education in Indonesia.

4 Conclusion

First, in Semarang District, it is urgent to carry out regrouping or school incorporation, especially focusing on small schools. That is a school with a ratio of <= 16 students per study group. Carry out multigrade learning models in small schools is necessary because regrouping is not possible due to the geographic condition. As well as empowering the Wiyata Bhakti teacher (non Civil Servant teacher). The number of Wiyata Bhakti teachers replacing the role of the shortage of Civil Servant teachers is quite significant. Therefore, efforts are to be made to optimize the Wiyata Bhakti teachers by empowering them by increasing their welfare through the District Budget.

Second, it is necessary to realize mutually beneficial cooperation between the Semarang District Education Office and the LPTK in implementing the PKB program. The materials that need to be collaborated to improve teacher professionalism are the use of ICT in learning, a mastery of subject matter related to the subjects taught by the teacher, a pedagogical which allows teachers to be better in conveying the subject matter to students, and the development of educational curriculum and technology. In this collaboration the LPTK provided its lecturers as resource persons and the Semarang District Education Office provided trainees, namely teachers, principals, and supervisors, as well as the costs of organizing training to improve teacher competencies.

Third, the experts from LTPK could have been the consultants for the Semarang District Education Office in preparing PKB planning systematically and fairly. Ranged from teacher competency mapping, training needs analysis, analysis of availability of education funds, stages of training implementation, to implementation of monitoring and evaluation. Monitoring and evaluation is to be carried out to determine the achievement of the objectives, the implementation of the PKB program and to know the outputs and outcomes of the PKB implementation in Semarang District.

References

1. Danim, S. 2011. *Pengembangan Profesi Guru: Dari Prajabatan, Induksi, Ke Profesional Madani*. Jakarta: Kencana.
2. Hendarsjah, Hidajat. 2009. *Sudah Pantaskah Biaya Pendidikan Anak Anda? Cara Sederhana untuk Menalar Alokasi Pembiayaan di Bidang Pendidikan. Jakarta:* Elex Media Komputindo.
3. National Center for Education Statistis. 2009. *Teachers' Use of Educational Technology in U.S. Public Schools*. http://nces.ed.gov/pubs2010/2010040.pdf diakses 8 Mei 2015.
4. Nurkolis dan Yovitha Yuliejantiningsih, 2015. *Efektivitas Implementasi Pengembangan Keprofesian Berkelanjutan*. Prosiding Seminar Nasional PGSD 2015. Semarang: Jurusan PGSD FIP Universitas PGRI Semarang. ISBN: 978-602-0960-13-5.
5. Seyfarth, John T. 2002. *Human Resources Management for Effective Schools*. Boston: Allyn and Bacon.
6. The World Bank. 2009. *Investing in Indonesia Education at the District Level: an Analysis of Regional Public Expenditure and Financial Management*. Jakarta: The World Bank.

Implementation of learning quality assurance based on applied education technology

Haryono, Heri Triluqman Budisantoso, *Edi* Subkhan, *Yuli* Utanto

Universitas Negeri Semarang, Indonesia

Abstract. This research aims to analyze the implementation of learning quality assurance at school and develop its model based on the applied educational technology. The research unit of analysis encompassing several junior high school, senior high school and vocational school in Semarang, Kendal, and Kudus district. The research results (1) school had implemented the learning quality assurance including the planning, implementation, monitoring, and evaluating process, although the documentation is still desultory, (2) the learning quality assurance based on the applied educational technology had been developed as a reference to define (a) the scope of quality assurance at school, (b) the quality policy and quality assurance organization at school, (c) the standard of learning quality and its achievement strategy, and (d) the manual for learning quality and its instrument, and (3) the learning quality assurance based on the applied educational technology is worth implemented on the learning quality assurance process at school.

1 Introduction

Quality of learning is needed to realize education that is able to produce students with better learning capacity. High quality learning will lead students either to acquire a number of knowledge, skills and attitudes, and the more important is to develop their learning capacity about how to gain knowledge, skills and attitudes (Zamroni, 2000; Semiawan, 1998). Therefore the quality of learning is needed as a dimension of benchmark for the professional development of educators as well as the development of schools as educational institutions that must consistently develop towards competition in the information age and openness of the world.

Related to the efforts of improving the learning quality that must be pursued by every professional educator, the presence of educational technology is an enlightenment. Educational technology as an area of interest with an effort to facilitate the learning process have some following characteristics; (1) give special attention and unique service from each of the target students, (2) use various kinds and as many learning resources as possible, and (3) apply a system approach (Miarso, 2002). Educating technology is not merely applying technology in education, but it is a systematic and systemic process to enhance the quality of education and learning processes. Although it is undeniable that in the system process it allows for the application of technology in the sense of the product.

Applied educational technology in the learning system, has the potential to improve the quality of learning that has an impact on student learning outcomes. Praxis of learning is inseparable from the application of educational technology. Quality learning can only be realized if it is properly designed, equipped with the necessary materials, presented through the appropriate media and resources, divide the roles clearly based on the functions between components, and properly assessed. This prerequisite is a field of educational technology work both theoretically and practically.

Regarding to the applied educational technology potential in improving the quality of learning, developing it as a learning quality assurance system in schools is necessary. As a quality assurance system, educational technology in schools must pay attention to the quality assurance system recently run in schools, and leads its system to be able to run more systematically, directed and organized.

The role of educational technology in assisting the implementation and development of a quality assurance system can be realized in the form of organizations that formally institutionalize in schools. This is needed so that the operational activities of the quality assurance system do not rely on the principal and the management team, but distribute the duty to the authorized person to conduct quality assurance of education and learning in schools. This is where the group or team given the authority to carry out the quality assurance process of learning in schools is formed in which it is consists of teachers and other education personnel, especially education technologists.

Technically operational and institutional structure of the implementation of learning quality assurance systems in schools, can refer to the idea of prototyping the educational technology development team developed by Budiyono, et al. (2014). The education technology development team in this case can be used as an institution that is formally exist in the school, in addition to other institutions such as guidance and counseling (BK). The basis for this institutional development is Regulation of the Minister of Administrative Reform (Permenpan) No. PER / 2 / M.PAN / 3/2009 concerning functional positions of learning technology and credit numbers. With the existence of a clear institutional structure, the application of educational technologists as a learning quality assurance system can be assessed, developed, implemented and evaluated for improvement.

Empirically there are many research which study have given contribution to the efforts of improving the learning quality. Several researches on educational technology from the dimensional process can be stated as follows. Haryono (1997) developed a learning process model characterized by an increase in creative and critical thinking skills that were significantly able to improve the ability to think creatively and critically of elementary students in Central Java. Haryono (2006) developed a science process skills-based learning model to improve students' scientific abilities which included dimensional product, process, and attitude. Development and implementation of mathematics learning designs that integrate the growth of vocational skills among junior high school students developed by Susento (2011). Online learning development based on e-pedagogical principles developed by Nugraha (2011). While Budiono, et al. (2014) develop an applied educational technology in improving the quality of learning in the form of learning technology developer assistance in education units.

2 Methods

In accordance with the research target, which is to produce a learning quality assurance model or system based on applied educational technology, research is carried out with the approach of "development research". The research program is followed up with the development for improvement or refinement of a practice (Borg and Gall, 1989: 784-5). The study begins with an assessment of the implementation of learning quality assurance in schools. Based on the factual model of learning quality assurance run in school and the results of literature review, developed (formulated) systems or models of quality assurance of the learning process as intended. The product produced was tried to be implemented in the implementation of learning quality assurance in schools, to know the level of feasibility and effectiveness as a learning quality assurance system or model in schools.

With a focus on developing and testing learning quality assurance systems based on applied educational technology, research was conducted at 8 schools, namely 3 (three) Junior High Schools, 2 (two) Senior High Schools, 2 (two) Vocational Schools, and 1 (one) Madrasah Aliyah in Semarang City, Kendal Regency, and Kudus Regency. Data is collected by questionnaire techniques, interviews, and focused discussions. The questionnaire technique was carried out to get data of the implementation of quality assurance in schools and the implementation of learning quality assurance systems based on applied education technology in general. Interviews and focused discussions were conducted to explore data quality assurance systems based on applied education technology more intensely, about various substantive and technical aspects of implementation in the field. Data analysis was carried out in a descriptive quantitative manner.

3 Results and Discussion

The results and discussion of the findings of this study are outlined in 3 main points as follows.

3.1 Quality assurance of learning in schools

Learning quality assurance in schools is the process of how schools make efforts to ensure that the learning process that takes place in schools meets the quality standards as promised. In this study the focus of learning quality assurance is directed at aspects of learning plans, learning implementation, monitoring and evaluation of learning.

The results of the quantitative data shows that the implementation of learing quality assurance in schools is as follows.

Table 1. Profile of Implementation of Learning Quality Assurance in Schools

ASPECT OF LEARNING QUALITY ASSURANCE	AVERAGE SCORE	%
Learning plans quality standard	12,26	87,55
Learning plans quality achievement tools	9,69	80,77
Learning process implementation quality standard	11,87	84,82
Quality achievement tools of learning process implementation	12,29	87,75
Monitoring and evaluation standard of learning	7,02	87,76
Quality achievement tools of learning monitoring and evaluation	7,28	91,02

Reading Table 1 can be found that quantitatively the implementation of learning quality assurance in schools can be stated to be good. It means that generally schools have and or set learning quality standards both from the dimensions of planning, implementation of processes, monitoring and evaluation, and have been supported by the required quality achievement tools. In detail the general description of the learning quality assurance in schools can be explained as follows.

First, the quality standard for the planning of learning developed by the school, including; (1) preparation of syllabus, (2) preparation of learning implementation plans, (3) development of teaching materials, (4) selection and use of learning methods, (5) development of learning media, (6) development of student worksheets, and (7) development of measuring instruments for student learning success.

Second, supporting tools for achieving quality standards for learning planning developed and used by schools, including; (1) standard operational procedures (POS) preparation of learning planning, (2) instruments for monitoring learning planning, (3) availability of monitoring planning team exclude the Head and Deputy Principal, (4) presence audit or validation of learning planning documents, (5) reporting of the results of the learning planning audit, and (6) the follow-up program of the results of the learning planning audit.

Third, the quality standards for the implementation of the learning process developed by the school include; (1) the maximum time limit for the teacher to come late in class, (2) minimum time limit for the teacher to leave the class or end the lesson before the time is up, (3) the learning stage which includes the introduction, core and closing, (4) the use of learning strategies that encourage (stimulate) student-centered learning processes, (5) the selection and use of media that supports the achievement of student competencies, (6) the use of various assessment techniques to measure students' learning success, and (7) reporting students' learning result by teachers to students.

Fourth, supporting tools to achieve the quality of the learning process implementation developed and implemented in schools, including; (1) standard operational procedures (POS) for the implementation of learning, (2) monitoring instrumentsof learning implementation, (3) the monitoring team of learning implementation exclude the Head and Deputy Principal, (4) learning implementation journals which must be filled by the teacher according to the schedule, (5) audit or validation of teaching journals by the monitoring team, and follow-up program on the results of the audit of the learning implementation.

Fifth, quality standards for the implementation of learning monitoring and evaluation developed by schools include; (1) the time for monitoring and evaluating learning in schools, (2) the evaluation mechanism of learning by students, (3) reporting of the results of the learning process monitoring and evaluation, and (4) follow-up program on the result of the learning process monitoring and evaluation.

Sixth, supporting tools to achieve the quality of monitoring and evaluation of learning developed and used in schools including; (1) standard operating procedures (POS) of learning monitoring and evaluation, (2) instruments of learning monitoring and evaluation, (3) reporting of the results of learning monitoring and evaluation, and (3) follow-up programs on the results of monitoring and evaluation of learning.

Quantitatively, based on the score of the implementation of the learning quality assurance system, it has reached more than 80% in all aspects. This indicates that the learning quality assurance process has been carried out quite well. But another facts that need to be criticized is that there is no documents that records the quality assurance process of learning in school, and no written evidence regarding the learning quality assurance process. For this inconsistent phenomenon, it can be explained as follows.

First, principally, school have gained an awareness that high quality learning is the school's duties and responsibilities that must be realized. Management (Head and Deputy Principal), teachers, education staff together have been called upon to realize a quality learning process as a product of institutional performance. All school components will feel proud if they receive recognition and appreciation from the community and all stakeholders for the learning performance they are able to provide. For this matter, various efforts have been made by schools (including the quality assurance process) for the realization of quality learning services for students.

Second, the school's understanding of the concepts and application of quality control as an integrated quality management process towards sustainable quality improvement is incomplete and needs to be improved. Technically, schools are encouraged and forced to carry out educational quality assurance processes both internally and externally with the enactment of Minister of National Education Regulation No. 13 of 2009 concerning the Education Quality Assurance System (SPMP). But they tend to focus on administrative matter to achieve the categorical recognition status of the school. The technical mastery of education quality assurance itself seems to be the task and responsibility of the management, while the implementing component (teachers and education personnel) is only supporting the completeness of administrative documents.

Third, there is a misconception in providing an assessment or justification of the concept of quality learning. Most people, including actors and stakeholders of school education, have an understanding that quality learning is learning that can make students achieve their target to get high score in learning result, can be accepted at favorite schools or colleges. Such understanding is not entirely wrong, but it becomes unwise if the implications are not proportional, especially from the education actors in schools. It will be a wrong and misleading understanding, if quality learning is only interpreted as what most people understand. The quality learning process is not sufficiently understood when it is planned / prepared properly and then stops students being able to achieve good academic performance, then deems it to be a good or quality learning process.

3.2 The learning quality assurance system based on applied educational technology

Educational technology is an ethical study and practice in facilitating learning and improving performance through efforts to create, utilize and manage various processes and sources of technology appropriately (Januszeski, 2008). The learning quality assurance system is based on applied educational technology in the context of this study, including; (a) limitation and scope of learning quality assurance in schools, (b) quality and organizational policies, (c) quality standards of learning and achievement mechanisms, (d) learning quality manuals and instruments.

3.2.1 Limitation and scope of learning quality assurance in schools

Learning is the process of interacting students with educators and learning resources in a particular learning environment. In the context of learning schooling means the process of interaction between students and teachers and other learning resources in the learning environment at school. Referring to the Standards of the Learning Process as stipulated in Minister of National Education

Regulation No. 65 of 2013, learning is directed at achieving change in the cognitive, affective, psychomotor, and cooperative domains. The achievement of the cognitive realm refers to the ability with regard to knowledge, reasoning, and / or thought. Affective domain refers to the ability to prioritize different feelings, emotions, and reactions based on reasoning such as acceptance, participation, and attitude determination. Psychomotor domains point to abilities that prioritize physical skills, such as perception and creativity. The cooperative domain refers to the ability to work together, build networks, and work together with others.

In order to make the learning process developed by teachers in schools to be able to produce changes in all four domains in a balanced manner, and to produce graduates who meet the competency standards as determined in the curriculum and expectations of stakeholders, a quality standard of learning is required based on legislation, the vision and the mission of the school. Learning quality standards are measures and criteria that must be met in every learning process that takes place in schools, functioning as a form of learning quality assurance provided by schools to customers, namely students, parents, and other educational stakeholders. Learning quality standards in the context of this research are limited to learning planning, implementation of learning processes, monitoring and evaluation of learning.

The learning quality standards developed and determined by the school then become guidelines for the Principal, Deputy Principal, school learning quality assurance team, teachers, students, and education personnel in carrying out the learning quality assurance function in accordance with their respective roles. Referring to the quality standards of learning that are developed, the learning quality assurance system is directed at efforts to meet the standards of learning planning, implementation of learning, monitoring and evaluation of learning.

3.2.2 Quality policy and learning quality assurance organization in schools

The school organizes learning based on the awareness that students have unique talents, abilities, and personalities. Through student-centered learning as mandated by the 2013 Curriculum, schools responsible for helping students develop toward a complete personal achievement by mastering the field of science from existing subjects, having conscience, and compassion. Learning by standards as determined by the school is a promise to the stakeholders that must be realized by the teacher assisted by all relevant school components in accordance with their respective functions and roles.

The organizational structure of quality assurance in schools is regulated and determined by the school. Technically, the learning quality assurance system is under the responsibility of the Principal, controlled by the Deputy Principal for Curriculum and Learning, and is carried out operationally by the school learning quality assurance team. Teams or learning quality assurance groups are formed and assigned by schools to develop quality standards for learning in schools, develop manual quality attainment of learning standards and monitoring instruments, periodically monitor and evaluate the learning process in schools, report the results of monitoring and evaluation of learning implementation at school, and designing follow-up programs to improve the quality of learning in schools.

3.2.3 Learning quality standards and standard achievement mechanisms

The learning quality standard is a measure and or a benchmark for the quality or quality of learning in schools which includes planning, implementation, monitoring and evaluation.

Quality standards for learning planning, containing provisions that; (1) the teacher makes a learning implementation plan (RPP) based on the syllabus of subjects with a format standardized by the school, (2) the teacher chooses and determines learning strategies, methods, and techniques according to the subject characteristics by orienting on student-centered learning, (3) the teacher chooses, determines, designs, and makes learning media to support the success of the planned learning process, (4) the teacher develops materials or teaching materials in accordance with the competencies that will be achieved in learning, (5) teachers develop develop an instrument for assessing student learning outcomes.

Quality standards for the implementation of learning, containing provisions that; (1) the teacher must start and end the lesson with a certain time limit, (2) the teacher conducts learning activities according to the stages that must be passed (introduction, core, and closing, (3) the teacher in learning needs to make maximum use of learning resources and media , (4) teachers fill learning journals at the end of each learning hour.

Quality standard of learning supervision or commonly used terms of monitoring and evaluation, contain provisions that; (1) there is a monitoring and evaluation mechanism for learning carried out by authorized parties of the school, (2) monitoring and evaluation of learning carried out transparently within the framework of learning quality assurance, (3) the results of monitoring and evaluation are used as the basis for the development of learning quality improvement programs, (4) teachers use the results of monitoring and evaluation as a basis for self-reflection and improvement effort.

To meet the quality standards described above, the mechanism that is carried out is;

1) Learning planning, (a) The teacher prepares Learning Implementation Plan (RPP), develops teaching materials, develops learning media and measurement instrument of student learning outcomes. RPP and learning tools needed are developed (made) per basic competency (KD). (b) The team or learning quality assurance group or the party authorized by the school validates the learning planning developed by the teacher.
2) Implementation of learning, (a) Teachers carry out learning according to the schedule by implementing RPP that has been prepared in advance. (b) The teacher fills the learning implementation journal in the form provided by the school through the school

learning quality assurance team or group. (c) The team or school learning quality assurance group or the party authorized by the school validates the implementation of the learning carried out by the teacher.

3) Monitoring and evaluation of learning implementation, (a) The school quality assurance team or group or the party authorized by the school conducts periodic learning monitoring and evaluation, they are at the beginning of the semester, mid semester, and the end of the semester. (b) The school's teaching quality assurance team or group reports the results of periodic monitoring and evaluation in a forum attended by the Head and Deputy Principal, the school learning quality assurance team, teachers and related educational personnel. (c) The school learning quality assurance team together with the Deputy Principal in the field of curriculum and learning compiles a follow-up program on the results of the monitoring and evaluation in the form of learning quality improvement programs in schools. (4) Teachers utilize the monitoring and evaluation results as a material of self-reflection for further improvement.

3.2.4 Learning quality manual and instruments

Schools as formal education institutions besides being responsible for carrying out teaching in quality, but also must provide certainty and assurance that the learning held is truly high quality. For this reason the school needs to develop a quality learning manual as a reference and / or guideline for all learning activities ranging from planning, implementation, monitoring and evaluation. The learning quality manual contains the rationales for quality assurance of learning, school vision and mission, learning quality standards and mechanisms for achieving standards, quality policies and quality assurance organizations of school learning, and instruments of monitoring and evaluation.

The learning quality manual is developed based on the applicable laws and regulations specifically the Regulations of National Education Minister (Permendiknas) No. 65 of 2013 concerning the Standards of the Learning Process, combined with good learning practices that have been built in schools. Thus the quality manual is more documenting the practices exist in school, strengthened to facilitate the process of quality learning that must be carried out by the school. This quality learning manual developed later becomes a guideline and criteria for schools in providing an assessment of the learning performance carried out by the teacher.

The quality learning manual developed by the school is completed with an instrument of monitoring and evaluation as an integral part of the learning quality assurance in schools. This instrument is used in the quality learning audit process carried out by a team or school learning quality assurance group. The data collected through this instrument is the subject of reports of the team and it also becomes a material of self-reflection for the teacher.

The model of learning quality assurance system based on applied education technology comprehensively can be visualized in the flow chart as follows.

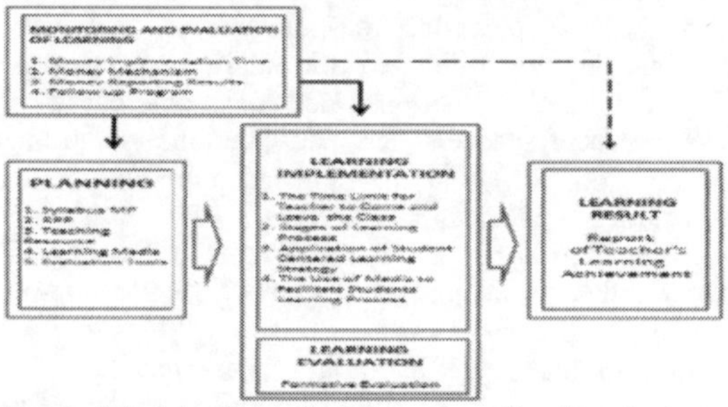

Fig. 1. Model of Applied Learning Quality Assurance System Based on Educational Technology

3.3 Implementation of learning quality assurance system based on applied educational technology

The implementation of learning quality assurance systems based on applied educational technology in the context of this study is explained from the dimensions of the application of the learning process standards and the feasibility of the system in the learning quality assurance process in schools.

The results of data analysis show that the level of application of the learning process standard in the school that implements the learning quality assurance system based on applied educational technology is summarized in Table 2 below.

Table 2. Application of Learning Process Standard in School

STANDARD ASPECT OF LEARNING PROCESS	AVERAGE SCORE	%
Encouraging students to gain curiosity	3,48	86,88
Based on various learning resources	3,48	86,88
Striving to Strengthen the scientific approach implementation	3,20	80,00
Competency based	3,39	84,87
Integrated Learning	3,30	82,50
Multi-dimensional Learning	2,97	74,34
Aiming to Applicative skills	3.30	82,50
Balancing improvement between hardskills and softskills.	3,28	81,80
Cultivation of students to become a lifetime learner	3,18	79,38
Application of exemplary values, gaining willingness, and developing students' creativity	3,48	86,88
Learning that takes place at home, school, and society	3,15	78,75

Applying principle that everyone is an educator, a student, and everywhere is a learning place	2,90	72,50
The use of Information and Communication Technology to improve learning effectiveness and efficiency	3,43	85,63
Acknowledgement of Individual and cultural background diversities of students	3,18	79,38
Total	45,38	81,03

In general, the application of the standard process in learning in the school that implements the quality assurance system of learning based on applied educational technology, can be stated as follows.
First, learning in schools has implemented the process standard quite well with average score achievement of 45.38 from the theoretic score of 56, which means it has reached 81.03%. Teachers at the school have attempted to implement teaching process standards as mandated by Minister of National Education Regulation No. 65 of 2013 in the practice of learning for their students.
Second, from a number of process standard components that must be implemented by the teacher in the learning process, components that encourage students to gain curiosity, based on various sources, applying values through exemplary, building willingness, and developing creativity, as well as utilizing information and communication technology in improving the effectiveness and efficiency of learning has been implemented in the teacher's learning practise. The average score has reached 3.4 from the theoretical score of 4, which means it has reached above 85%.
Third, beside the fact that a number of components of the process standard have been implemented very well, there are a number of components whose level of application needs to be improved because the achievement score is less than 3.0, which means less than 75%. Components that are lacking are kind of learning that must be able to provide multi-dimensional and learning-responsive opportunities that must be able to take place at school, at home, and in the community.
The feasibility of an applied quality assurance system for learning based on educational technology to be implemented in schools is concluded in Table 3 as follows.

Table 3. Feasibility of Learning quality assurance System based on Applied Educational Technology

DIMENSIONAL FEASABILITY	AVERAGE SCORE	%
Relevance of system with the schools' vision and mission which is oriented on quality achievement	3,25	81,25
Suitability of System function and school's objective which is oriented on quality achievement	3,00	75,00
Adequacy of system aspects with the field of quality learning in schools	2,98	74,38
Application of the system in the practice of learning quality assurance in school	2,80	70,00
The compatibility with the capacity of human resources in schools	2,78	69,38
The compatibility with learning infrastructure availability in school	2,75	68,75
Its Benefit for the management in controlling learning quality control in school	3.08	76,88
Its benefit for the teacher in learning performance improvement in school	3,13	78,13
The benefit for education personnel in the contribution of improving the learning quality	3,15	78,75
The benefit of the system for the learning quality achievement effort	3,05	76,25
The benefit of the system for the effort of learning quality culture development in school achievement effort	3,10	77,50
Total	33,05	75,11

From Table 3 can be seen that in principle the learning quality assurance system based on applied educational technology developed can be said to be suitable for its use or implementation. The average score of system feasibility of reached 33.05 or 75.11% of the theoretical score of 44. This indicates that the system that is built is relevant to the vision, school, and school objectives that are oriented towards achieving quality, containing the fields of learning quality assurance in schools, can be applied in practice, useful for the efforts of achieving the learning quality in schools.
Learning quality assurance systems based on applied educational technology are substantially assessed by respondents to have a high relevance to the vision and mission of schools that are oriented towards the achievement of learning quality. The system built has a high value for management (Principal) in the framework of learning quality control in schools, for teachers in maintaining and improving their learning performance, and for educational staff in contributing to the learning quality achievement in schools. In addition, the system built also has the potential to build a quality culture in the school environment.
Learning quality assurance system based on educational technology is a form of real contribution in educational technology in improving the quality of learning in schools. As an application of the concept of educational technology that is still in the process of development, at the level of implementation in schools requires commitment and willingness together with all

components of the school. Achieving school quality, the quality of learning is not enough to be carried out only by some components, but requires the contribution of all components according to their respective functions and roles. Assignment of duties and responsibilities explicitly in the organizational structure, the existence of actor who implement the learning quality assurance process in schools is an agenda and prerequisites for more efficient system implementation.

Conclusion

Principally the school has carried out learning quality assurance, has quality learning standards, operational standards procedures for achieving quality, and a system of monitoring the achievement of quality learning. There is an unwritten reference that must be met by the teacher and the school quality assurance team in achieving the determined learning quality.

The learning quality assurance system based on applied educational technology is developed within a frame of reference that contains limits and scope for learning quality assurance in schools, quality policies and organization of learning quality assurance in schools, learning quality standards and mechanism in which it affects the improvement of the learning quality in schools. As an applied system in educational technology which is not final and is a large-scale and broad-scale idea, it still needs further development to be more implementable and have an impact on improving the quality of learning in schools.

The learning quality assurance system based on applied educational technology is principally feasible to be implemented as a model in the learning quality assurance process in schools. The implementation of the learning quality assurance model based on applied education technology in schools has an impact on reaching the learning standard of learning quality.

References

1. Bahagia, Putra Johan. 2011. "Pening-katan Hasil Belajar melalui Pembelajaran Kooperatif Model Jigsaw dengan Alat Peraga pada Siswa kelas V". *Jurnal Penelitian dan Pemikiran Pendidikan (JP3)*, Volume 1, Nomor 1. September 2011.
2. Budiyono, Haryono, dan Hardjono. 2014. "Pengembangan Imple-mentasi teknologi Pendidikan dalam Peningkatan Kualitas Pembelajaran di Sekolah". *Laporan Penelitian* (tidak diterbitkan). Semarang: LP2M Unnes.
3. Delors, Jacques. 1996. *Learning: The Treasure Within*. Paris: UNESCO.
4. Ditjen Dikti Kemdikbud. 2011. *Peningkatan Kualitas Pembelajaran*. Jakarta: Direktorat Pendidik dan Tenaga Kepen-didikan.
5. Fibonacci, Anita. 2012. "Peningkatan Hasil Belajar IPA Siswa Kelas X TKR 1 SMKN 7 Semarang melalui Joyful Learning Menggunakan Game Guess My Word". *Jurnal Penelitian Pendidikan*. Volume 29, No. 2 Oktober 2012.
6. Haryono. 2014. "Terapan Teknologi Pendidikan dalam Praksis Kurikulum 2013: Optimalisasi Peran Jabatan Fungsional Pengembang Teknologi Pembelajaran". *Proceeding 2014 Educational International Seminar: "Strengthening Teachers & Educational Personnel Competence in Scour Change"*. Padang, November 22th to 24th 2014.
7. Januszewski, Alan. 2001. *Educational Technology, The Development of a Concept*. Englewood, Colorado: Libraries Unlimited.
8. Januszewski, Alan and Michael Molenda. 2008. *Educational Technology: A Definition with Commentary*. New York: Taylor & Francis Group.
9. Miarso, Yusufhadi. 2002. "Konsep dan Terapan Teknologi Pembel-ajaran", Makalah dalam Kuliah Perdana Mahasiswa S2 TP UNNES, 14 September 2002.
10. Miarso, Yusufhadi. 2004. *Menyemai Benih Teknologi Pendidikan*. Jakarta: Prenada Media.
11. Romiszowski, A.J. 1989. *Designing Instructional System*. London: Kogan Page.
12. Salisbury. 2002. *Instructional Technology, Past, Present, and Future*. Englewood, Colorado: Libraries Unlimited.
13. Semiawan, Conny R. 1998. *Pendidikan Tinggi: Peningkatan Kemampuan Manusia Sepanjang Hayat Seoptimal Mungkin*. Jakarta: Ditjen Dikti Depdikbud.
14. Sugiyono. 2009. *Metode Penelitian Pendidikan: Pendekatan Kuantitatif, Kualitatif, dan R & D*. Bandung: Alfabeta.
15. Zamroni. 2000. *Paradigma Pendi-dikan Masa Depan*. Yogyakarta: Bigraf Publishing

English Grammar On 2013 Curriculum: The Development of Game Based Learning Multimedia

Budi Setiawan, Asrowi
Doctoral Program of Education, Teacher Training and Education Faculty, Universitas Sebelas Maret, Indonesia

Abstract. This Research is aimed to find out the effectiveness of game based learning multimedia in order to gain student learning outcomes on English subject with the topic of grammar in the classroom. The research development of multimedia game based learning using the procedure of Raiser and Demsey consisting of 5 stages namely: 1) Analysis which covers needs and theoretical analysis, 2) Design which includes Core and basic competence's identification, material's selection and submission, flowchart and story board arrangement, 3) Develop that contains production, media and material's experts validation and students' responses and product's trial after the revision done. 4) Implement that covers the final product's application towards the experiment class, 5) Evaluate becoming the last stage of all by having a test for both classes which are control and experiment class to see whether is there any differences between the class applying the multimedia game based learning and not. The trial of product development tested had passed several processes covering; the review from media's expert which includes software changes and visual communication, the review from content's expert covers material and instructional design, students' responses towards products' usage and attractiveness, small group and big group test trial. The result showed that the students at the control class taught by conventional way as in speech has less motivation and lower score compared with the experiment class applying interactive multimedia game based learning. There is an interaction between learning media and learning motivation those effects on students' learning achievement especially in English grammar. Thus, it can be said that the result of the development of multimedia game based learning is effective to improve students learning outcomes.

Keywords: *Multimedia, game based learning, grammar, learning outcomes*

1 Introduction

Curriculum change will have a rational impact on the adjustment and change of various standards existed in a curriculum which has been designed and defined including the competence standard, this change is specifically shown from Curriculum 2006 (KTSP) into Curriculum 2013 (K-13). There are both direct and indirect effects as a sustainable impact caused from a result of the policy. Based on its function, the purpose of teaching English includes: (1) Developing the ability to communicate in the language both spoken and written including listening, speaking, reading, and writing; (2) Arising awareness of the essence and importance of English as a foreign language to become the main media for learning; (3) Creating the comprehension about interrelationship between language and culture as well as expanding cultural horizons so that students have cross-cultural insights and willingness to involve themselves in cultural diversity.

As well as in English subjects, based on the distribution of content that refers to syllabus, there are differences in the inclusion of grammar or grammar skills in English subjects for tenth graders of senior high school. In English, grammar has a particular pattern that varies according to the context of the time. Consequently, it will cause difficulties for students especially when the learning process of the learner is not well-facilitated by the size of the portion from the teacher to deliver the basic concept of grammar through teacher-centered. On the other hand, curriculum 2013 makes students to be more active in all aspects with smaller portion of teachers to take control in the process of teaching and learning activities. As a result, a short-term effect that can be seen directly is students' confusion and lack of understanding of the basic concept of sentence patterns in an English language. Moreover, it also offers major implications in the cognitive or academic achievement of these students.

The role of teachers in choosing and determining learning materials or teaching materials becomes very important in solving learners' problems especially in learning activities. As a hereditary culture for many educators nowadays, in this case the teacher in particular, still apply conventional methods or techniques in teaching and learning activities. Most of educators have weakness in utilizing teaching materials and learning media because of their lack of innovation.

Nowadays, in millennial generation era people are forced to be *global citizen*. It means that all aspects must be related to computerization spreaded out almost in all

* Corresponding author: bububaba381@gmail.com

areas of human life. Even the world of education is also connected to the computer invasion or commonly called as *digital world*. Furthermore, this digital era have people be creative in developing learning materials using computers as a source of learning besides books. According to Simonson & Thomson (1994: 147), Computer Assisted Learning is effective in improving student mastery in all levels of education, highly effective in improving student mastery at primary school level continuing at intermediate to tertiary level and also can save the time for learning.

Encouraged by Yusuf Hadi Miarso (2005: 45) that learning developed or assisted by computer was able to increase students' motivation and their absorption capacity of the subject matter. This is because computer-assisted learning method is able to cultivate motivation for students to be more comprehensive with material presented, add realism to conduct work exercises,, and be able to stimulate students in responding learning materials to improve thier learning achievement.

The use of media that is still conventional becomes a crucial factor which requires to be upgraded and not only relies on a medium which is a book. It needs innovation in presenting teaching materials in other interactive forms that are able to attract students' enthusiasm and activeness, one of them is through computer-based interactive learning.

Thornburry (2002: 1) states "*Traditionally, grammar has been almost exclusively with analysis at the level of the sentence. Thus grammar is a description of the rules that govern a language's sentence are formed*". Meanwhile, grammar is related to sentence levels and pictures of rules governing the formation of a sentence in the language. In this case, the focus is more on the sentence and how to shape it. Meanwhile, according to Ur (2009: 75), grammar in general is sometimes defined as the way words are put together to make correct sentences. This opinion has similarities previously expressed by Thornburry which relates to the rules on how the sentence is compiled completely. Another definition stated by Harmer (2006: 18), he explains that "*communicative competence involves knowing how to use the grammar and vocabulary of the language to achieve communicative goals, and knowing how to do this in a socially appropriate way*". Grammar is related to knowledge and skills: how to recognize grammar examples when it is spoken, how to identify it in writing, how to make them both in spoken and written form, how to understand its meaning based on the context, and produce meaningful sentences in its use.

Grammar is one of the language components besides pronunciation, spelling and vocabulary. It becomes very essential as a means of communication. Suyanto (2007: 43) reveals that grammar consists of patterns and rules of language that should be learned if we want to speak English properly. Richards (2008: 145) emphasizes that "*structure is still important to be taught in teaching English,*" he furthermore says that "*now teaching structure has controversial issues in teaching English, but in recent years, grammar teaching has regained its rightful place in language curriculum*". Teaching grammar is still considered important especially in teaching and learning activities as a means of communication. Additionally, a language will be grateful if it has the right grammar.

Smaldino, Lowther, & Russell (2007: 6) ever stated that *media* is plural form of *medium*, which is a means of communication. This term refers to anything that can bring information from source to receiver. While according to Sri Pudjiastuti (1999: 2) the media is a case that can distribute the message from sender to receiver so that it can stimulate the thoughts, feelings, attention, and interests of students in such a way that the learning process occurs. According to Hackbarth (1996: 229), multimedia is defined as a combined use of some media in conveying information in the form of text, graphics or animated graphics, movies, video and audio. Multimedia using computer-based includes hypermedia and hypertext. Hypermedia is a use of multimedia presentation format which includes text, silent graphics or animated graphics, movie and audio formats. Hypertext is a form of text, static diagram, images and tables that are displayed and arranged in a nonlinear way (sequence or line).

Roblyer (2003: 164) states multimedia or combination media is a medium consisting of still images, sounds, motion videos, animations and text that are combined in a product that aims to provide information. Rob Philip (1997: 8) states multimedia is a combination of text, image, sound, animation and video; some or all components are incorporated into a coherent program. As Munir (2008: 234) states that multimedia presentation can be interpreted as a technology that optimizes the role of the computer as media that display text, sound, graphics, video, animation in a view that is integrated and interactive.

Computers become the primary media for presentation of multimedia programs. Components in the computer are able to display a perfect combination of audio and visual integrative and slick in one program. Impressions of interaction created become very natural because of giving the opportunity by the users to be engaged in these activities. Games are an entertaining and interesting activity, tend to challenge, and also an activity in which learners can play and interact with each other. According to Wright et al (2006: 3), "*competition against others is not essential ingredient for games, but challenge is*". In choosing and describing the game, it is good to minimize competition, winners and losers, and maximize challenges, where everyone feels inspired and enthusiastic to start playing and doing their best. Generally, video games are any type of games played with computer devices and in the form of video display.

Media used can be through computer, cell phone, or game console. Those insights are general concepts that reflect our general understanding of the term "digital game" which does not mention all the complex components in it. According to ProActive: Fostering teachers' creativity through Game-Based Learning (2009), here are some characteristics or features of good-quality video games, favored by the general public and interesting among others; *Conflict, Goal and Rules, Short Feedback Cycles, Immersion and Engagement, Challenge, Adaptability, Replayability, Reward System, Competition*. The digital games are conditioning players in an unlimited world to explore without intervention from instructors. In this point, video games is an ideal medium for promoting real learning and a *learning-by-doing* process that can transform learners to be leaders of themselves in their learning experience. Hence, digital games are able to provide a meaningful learning experience by stimulating the interaction that a professional finds in the realm of real-world, where they can directly face related problems.

Based on the research problems mentioned above, the purpose of this study is to find the needs of teachers and students about multimedia for learning English, find procedures development of multimedia learning on the subject matter of an English grammar and find the effectiveness of learning by utilizing multimedia learning on an an English grammar for tenth graders senior high school.

2 Methods

This research is classified as developmental research or usually called R&D (Research and Development). Research and Development is a process or steps to develop a new product or refine an existing product. The meaning of the product in this context is not only the hardware but also the software. The research has been done in SMAN 3 Sragen. This research was conducted in English subjects in grade ten. The population of the research is all students Furthermore, this study held in second semester of academic year 2017/2018 by involving four different classes, which are product trial class, experimental class, experiment class and control class. Besides, the research development procedure consists of two stages: developing the model product and testing the quality and /or the effectiveness of the product (Sukardjo and Sari, 2009: 66). In developmental research, there is known one of the development models called ADDIE model.

The ADDIE model is an easy-to-use model in which the process used is systematic with a clear framework that produces effective, creative, and efficient products (Raiser and Demsey, 2007: 25). The ADDIE development model is a model of instructional design based on an effective and efficient system approach and an interactive process, for example: the evaluation of each phase can lead to the development of learning to the next phase. The final result of this phase is the initial product for the next phase. This model consists of 5 phases which are 1) Analysis, 2) Design, 3) Development, 4) Implementation, and 5) Evaluation.

3 Result And DIscussion

Multimedia Game-Based Learning

The development of products used as multimedia learning has been through several stages including production, validation of media experts, material expert validation and product trial. Here is the final model of the multimedia.

Figure 1. Games Opening

Figure 2. Games direction

Figure 3. Wrong answer respond

Figure 4. Correct answer respond

After the product has been declared feasible and tested, then the next step was to test the effectiveness of the product or called with the *t-test* by first performing the prerequisite test analysis. In test requirements analysis, it performed data analysis to test the hypothesis with t-test, then first test prerequisite analysis between classes which applied *game based learning* and classes which did not apply the same. The test requirements analysis is as follows.

3.1 Normality test

Normality test was conducted to determine the sample used in this study comes from the population with normal distribution or not. Kolmogrov smirnov test with $\alpha = 0.050$ and assisted with SPSS 16 program. H_o stated that the sample comes from a normally distributed population, if the significant value of the normality test is more than α (sig> 0,050) and $D_{count} < D_{table}$ then H_o is accepted. Normality test results in this study were as follows.

Table 1. *Pretest* Normality Test of the Experiment Class and the Control Class

	Class	Significant Value
Score	Control	.085
	Experiment	.060

Based on table 1, it can be seen that the significant value of normality test was more than α (sig> 0,05), in experiment class 0,060> 0,050 and in control class 0,085> 0,050, so it can be concluded that cognitive value of *pretest* experiment class and the control class was normally distributed.

Table 2. *Post test* of Normality test in Experimental and Control Class

	Class	Significant Value
Score	Control	.060
	Experiment	.126

Based on Table 2, it showed that the significant value of the normality test is more than α (sig> 0,050), in the experimental class 0.126> 0.050 and the control class normality test 0.60> 0.050, so it can be concluded that the cognitive value of pretest experimental class and the control class is also normally distributed.

3.2 Homogeneity Test

Homogeneity test was conducted to find out whether the data variance obtained between the tested groups was different or not. The method used was Levene's test with $\alpha = 0.050$. H_o stated that each group did not have the same variance. The decision of this test was that if the sig value of the homogeneity test is higher than α (sig> 0.050) then H_o was accepted, and it means homogeneous. The homogeneity test results in this study were as follows.

Table 3. Pretest Homogeneity Test of Experiment Class and Control Class

Levene Statistics	dfl	df2	Significant Value
Score	1	62	.139

Based on Table 3, it is known that Levene's Test significance value is 0.139. The value is higher than 0.05, so it can be concluded that the pretest cognitive values between the experimental and control classes has a homogeneous variance.

Table 4. Posttest Homepage Test of Experiment and Class Control

Levene Statistics	dfl	df2	Significant Value
Score	1	62	.576

Based on Table 4, it is known that Levene's Test significance value is 0.576. The value is higher than 0.05, so it can be concluded that the posttest cognitive value between the experimental class and the control class has a homogeneous variance.

3.3 Hypothesis Testing

In this study, testing the effectiveness and hypothesis used a test. Testing the hypothesis with t-test was utilized to test the effectiveness of game-based learning. The criterion used in taking the hypothesis is $\alpha = 0,05$. H_o is rejected if the probability significance (sig) < α (0.050) and if the probability significance level (sig) is > α (0.050) then H_o is accepted. The complete results of the test of effectiveness as well as hypothesis in this study are as follows.

Table 5. t-test Pretest of Experimental and Control Class

	Class	Mean
Score	Control	56,00
	Experiment	55,91

Based on Table 5, it can be seen that the mean or average value of the pretest of the control class is 56 and the experimental class is 55.91. This result indicates that the value of the control class learning outcomes is higher than the experimental class. However, to prove whether there is a significant difference between control class learning outcomes and the experimental class is presented in the table below.

Table 6. Test t-test (Independent samples test) pretest Control and Experimental Class

	T count	Significant
Score	.062	.951

Based on Table 6, it can be seen that the significance value of t-test is 0.951. The value of significance is higher than 0.05 which means that H_o is accepted. In addition, the value of t_{count} is equal to 0,062 $< t_{table}$ which is equal to 1,669. This result shows no significant difference for the mean of student learning outcomes between experimental and control class.

Table 7. Posttest Mean Value of Experimental and Control Class

	Class	Mean
Score	Control	64,44
	Experiment	71,66

Based on table 7, it can be seen that the posttest mean or average value of the experimental class is 71.66 and the control class is 64.44. It describes that the value of the students' experimental class learning outcomes is higher than control class. However, to prove whether there is a significant difference between the experimental class learning results and the control classes is presented in the table below.

Table 8. t-test (Independent samples test) Posttest Experimental and Control Class

	T count	Significant
Score	4.294	.000

Based on table 8, it can be seen that the significance value of t-test is 0.000. The value of significance is less than 0.05 which means that H_1 is accepted. Furthermore, the value of t_{count} is 4.294> table that is equal to 1.669. It shows that there is a significant difference mean of student learning outcomes between experimental and control class. This also proves that students' learning outcomes of experimental class is better than the control class.

The results of this research data that has been described above has a positive correlation with previous theories and / or results of previous research related to the use of media for improving students' achievement. Multimedia products used can be concluded effective in supporting and facilitating students in academic achievement in cognitive, affective and psychomotor domains. Learning with multimedia that combines audio and visual in this specific game is able to stimulate the activity, interest as well as attention of students on certain subject matter in a learning activity. In line with statement from Sri Pudjiastuti (1999: 2) that media is anything that can deliver the message from the sender to the receiver of the message so that it can stimulate the thoughts, feelings, attention, and interests of students in learning process. Followed and supported by Arsyad (2011: 26) that learning media can clarify the presentation of messages and information so that it will facilitate and improve the process and learning outcomes. The same opinion that supports that statement comes from Rudi et al (2009: 127) which explains that multimedia has some characteristics that are generally able to provide a solid learning tool for students such as self instructional, self contained, stand alone, and user friendly (easy to be operated). Additionally, this theory is appropriate and reinforced by Vaughan (2008: 6) which suggests that the use of multimedia is able to provide changes in student attitudes toward learning activities from passive learner into active learner with learning by doing (emphasize more on experience). The role of the teacher is also more likely to be a guide or facilitator of learning and to make students as main characters especially in student-centered activities.

Several previous studies have also supported the results of research presented above. Those are the results of the study by Chen et al (2015) on *The Comparison of Solitary and Collaborative Modes of Game-Based Learning on Students' Science Learning and Motivation* shows that games both individual and in groups do not show any difference in achievement of learning outcomes. This proves that games either independent or together are able to provide significant improvements from pretest to posttest. Hereafter, the result of the research describes that experiencing games in learning can improve students' enthusiasm in overall learning process. Last but not least, the results also show that games can encourage implicit exploration of science.

4. Conclusion

Learning process tends to focus more on lectures or teacher-centered. Supporting facilities only in the form of teaching materials such as books obtained from the school as a handbook with materials that seem concise and only cover the outline on each subject. With only use limited media images at times, so that students are less interested. Students require additional media or media support for helping them in learning and understanding the subject matter that teachers deliver in schools. Teachers have a big responsibility as the sources of information for students. On the other hand, schools have adopted and implemented curriculum 2013 which focuses more on a scientific approach and the learning process is based more on students or commonly referred to as student-centered. The application of multimedia game-based learning as a learning media is positively correlated to students' achievement and their learning attitudes. This can be seen from the improvement of student achievement at the time of pretest and posttest as well as their higher motivation to understand the lesson.

References

1. Arsyad, Azhar. *Media Pembelajaran*. Jakarta: PT Raja Grafindo Persada (2011)
2. Chen, C.-H., Wang, K.-C., & Lin, Y.-H, *The Comparison of Solitary and Collaborative Modes of Game-based Learning on Students' Science Learning and Motivation. Educational Technology & Society*, 18 (2), 237–248 (2015)
3. Hacbarth, S, *The educational technology handbook*. New Jersey: Educational Technology Publications Inc (1996)
4. Harmer, Jeremy. *How To Teach Grammar*. London. Longman (2006)
5. Heinich, Molenda, Russell, and Smaldino. . *Instructional Media and Technologies for Learning*. Prentice-Hall, Inc. New Jersey: Upper Saddle River. (2007)
6. Miarso, Yusuf Hadi. (2005). *Menyemai Benih Teknologi Pendidikan*.Jakarta: Kencana Prenada Media Group.
7. Munir. (2008). *Multimedia Konsep dan Aplikasi dalam Pendidikan*. Bandung: Alfabeta.
8. Phillips, R. (1997). *The developer's Handbook to Interactive Multimedia: A Practical Guide for Educational Applications*. London: Kogan Page.
9. Raiser, R.A & Dempsey, J.V. (2007). *Trends and Issues in Instructional Design and Technology*.

Secon Edition. New Jersey: Pearson Merril Prentice Hall.

10. Richards, J.C. (2008). *Methodology in Language Teaching. An Anthology of Current Practice.* New York: Cambridge University Press.
11. Roblyer, M.D. (2003). *Integrating Educational Technology into Teaching* (3rd ed) New Jersey. Merril Prentice Hall.
12. Rudi Susilana & Cepi Riyana. (2009). *Media Pembelajaran*. Bandung: CV Wacana Prima..
13. Simonson & Thomson. (1994). *Instructional Technology: The Definition and Domains of the Field*. Washington DC: AECT.
14. Sri Poedjiastoeti. (1999). *Media Pembelajaran*. Surabaya: Unipres Unesa.
15. Sukardjo dan Lis Permana Sari. (2009). *Metodologi Penelitian Pendidikan Kimia*.
16. Yogyakarta: FMIPA UNY.
17. Supartono Widyosiswoyo. (1996). *Ilmu Budaya Dasar*. Jakarta: Ghalia Indonesia.
18. Sutrisno. (2005). *Revolusi Pendidikan di Indonesia*. Yogyakarta: Ar Ruzz.
19. Suyanto, Kasihani K.E. (2007). *English for Young Learners*. Jakarta: Bumi Aksara
20. Tay Vaughan. (2008). *Multimedia: Making It Work.* New York: Mc Graw Hill.
21. Thornburry. S. (2002). *How To Teach Grammar*. Harlow, Essex: Pearson Education Limited
22. Ur, Penny. (2009). *A Course in Language Teaching Practice and Theory*. Cambridge University Press.
23. Chen, C.-H., Wang, K.-C., & Lin, Y.-H, The Comparison of Solitary and Collaborative Modes of Game –based Learning on Students' Science Learning and Motivation. Educational Technology & Society, 18 (2), 237- 248 (2015).
24. Wright. A, Betteridge. D, and Buckby. M. *Games For Language Learning. Third Edition*. Cambridge University Press (2006)
25. _______ *ProActive: Fostering teachers' creativity through Game-Based Learning* (2009)
26. Holl, B.G. Orr, Eur. Phys. J. E **14**, 7 (2004)
27. M. Ben Rabha, M.F. Boujmil, M. Saadoun, B. Bessaïs, Eur. Phys. J. Appl. Phys. (to be published)
28. Luigi T. De Luca, *Propulsion physics* (EDP Sciences, Les Ulis, 2009)
29. F. De Lillo, F. Cecconi, G. Lacorata, A. Vulpiani, EPL, **84** (2008)

Analysis of parent's discriminant partnership in the success ofimplementation of good school governance

Luluk Elyana[1*], *Yuli* Utanto[2], *Ghanis Putra* Widhanarto[2], and *Yoris Adi* Maretta[2]

[1]Department of Early Childhood Education, Faculty of Education IKIP Veteran Semarang, Indonesia
[2]Department of Curriculum and Educational Technology, Faculty of Education, Universitas Negeri Semarang, Indonesia

Abstract. Early childhood education is a strong foundation in the effort to prepare young people to face academic competition at the next level. The purpose of this study is to analyze the discriminant factors of parental partnership which are the determining factors for the implementation of *good school governance.* The research method is quantitative with a survey approach through a questionnaire given to respondents to reveal the influence of parental partnership on *good school governance*. The results showed that the higher parental involvement, the greater the success factor of *good school governance*. This research is useful as a guide in making decisions about model selection and analysis of factors related to parental partnership in early childhood education.

1 Introduction

Education in Indonesia has a variety of types and functions, namely formal education, non-formal education and informal education. The three types of education have their respective roles according to the criteria and rules set by the government. Formal education is education that is taken formally in a structured and tiered institution or organization unit consisting of primary education, secondary education and higher education. Formal education is carried out by the government (state status) and foundations or organizations that have fulfilled the requirements (private status) while non-formal education is a path of education that is obtained not formally through schools or universities, but still has a structure and tiered. Understanding informal education is a path of independent education obtained from families and the environment with a form of independent learning activities. The results of informal education pathways can be recognized if students can pass exams in accordance with national education standards organized by government-appointed institutions. (Siddik, 1984: 54)
Early Childhood Education (PAUD) is the level of education before the level of primary education, is a coaching effort aimed at children from birth to six years of age carried out through the provision of educational stimuli to help physical growth and development as well as spiritually so that children have readiness to enter further education, which is held on the formal, non-formal, and informal paths (Sujiono, 2009: 45). The age range of Indonesian early childhood is 0 - 6 years according to the National Education System Law No. 20 of 2003, with the continuous and continuous scope of development and growth processes being the benchmark for the success of subsequent child development.
The awareness of parents in stimulating their children's education in pre-kindergarten age is relatively low. This is due to the many pre-Kindergarten education services that have not been reached by the public whether it concerns the distance or cost issues. The existence of Pos PAUD as a form of Similar PAUD Unit (SPS) is intended to bridge these needs. The implementation of Pos PAUD can be integrated with the services of the Toddler Family Development (BKB) and Integrated Service Post (Posyandu). PAUD posts are intended for people who are not ready to involve their children in more intensive ECD services both for reasons of busy parents in school and other factors.
PAUD post is one of the government programs in early childhood education services and is part of SPS (Similar PAUD Unit). PAUD posts are managed by cadres consisting of housewives and mothers of the PKK driving team. The cadres become the foundation of controlling the institution's management wheel. Cadres and *stakeholders* villagein this case are the PKK mobilizing team trying to manage the performance of the institution's management. One of the objectives of the establishment of Pos PAUD is to provide educational playgrounds for early childhood children who are not served by other PAUD and give examples to parents and families about ways to stimulate early childhood education to continue at home. The PAUD Post Program is intended to provide PAUD services that can reach the wider community to rural areas. (DG PAUDNI, 2013: 17).
Early Childhood Education includes the PAUD Post in its management performance must understand PAUD management standards, where the implementation refers to the standards of content, processes, educators and education personnel, facilities and infrastructure, and financing. The implementation of managerial functions in Early Childhood Education includes Program Planning, Organizing, Implementation of Work Plans and Supervision (Government Regulation No. 137 of 2014). Program planning is the preparation of PAUD institution activities in achieving the vision, mission, goals of the institution. Each unit or program has a curriculum, educational calendar, organizational structure, discipline, and code of ethics. Formulating the school's vision and mission in the sense of formulating a vision, articulating a vision, communicating and building

a sense of belonging, evaluating and modifying the vision. In addition to formulating a vision is to make policies, design programs, determine and provide resources and modify policies and plans when needed.

Building the trust of parents of students begins with a partnership. A controlled and beneficial relationship for each party. The partnership is built by providing understanding to parents of students or caregivers that the role of caregivers is very important as the first and foremost support of the learning process wherever the institution is located.

Not all parents give full support. Parents' concerns arise when their children learn with an atmosphere different from PAUD in general. For example, when the PAUD Post receives children who have obstacles in their growth and development, parents of normal children have not fully given up and understand that their children learn together with different children. Many parents react negatively including waiting for their children to study every day, being protective of their children and being too intervened with decisions taken by the school. Another example, the learning orientation that parents want is in the context of reading, writing and calculating (calistung). This is contrary to the stimulation of child development that should be from *Developmentally Appropriate Practice* (DAP), namely the development of children who should be, Bredecamp (1987: 97).

Schools or Educational Institutions are basically a Public Institution, where people give their trust in education. The existence of public trust in schools or educational institutions is a mandate that must be managed properly. This is stated in the principles of *Good School Governance* (GSG). The essence of GSG is thatis *governance* defined as the mechanism, practice and procedures of the government and citizens regulating resources and solving public problems (Sumarto, 2009: 1). Although it is used in governance, it is important to be applied in the education world. The context of *governance* in this case is the *school's good school governance* is a container in realizing good management performance, while other factors involved in it namely the role of leader, parent partnership and overseer partnerships are actors who each determine the success of a performance .

The role of leadership in *good school governance is* found in research conducted by Bungai (2008) on "Increasing Equity, Quality, Relevance, Governance and Accountability of Kindergarten Education" in the *Journal of Educational Sciences.* Vol. 15: 74-81. This qualitative research found that the obstacle in leadership is the intervention of the foundation that overshadows so that it impedes the performance of school management. The intervention of the foundation is transparency in the financial / school budget.

Next is the study of Ko J. (2016) on The Development of School Autonomy and Accountability in Hong Kong: Multiple Changes in Governance, Work, Curriculum, and Learning, in the *International Journal of Educational Management*, Vol. 30: 1207. He explained his findings, namely leadership in *good school governance,* the principal is a change agent that is most influential in shaping the strategic direction of the school. The potentially transformative role of school principals has proven effective in terms of schools restructuring and improving schools in terms of shaping and developing a positive and energetic organizational culture.

Wang (2013: 671) in his research on parental involvement in Hong Kong stated that the findings they obtained in this study were four phases of development of how parents were included in school governance conceptualized together. Parents as guests who can come to school at any time and have separate responsibilities, parents as volunteers who have an encouraging role to participate, parents as clients through an accountability approach and parents as school committees together with managers have responsibility for help school progress.

Ralph B. McNeal Jr. (2014) said Researchers focus on parental involvement to focus on the relationship of student involvement and performance in isolation from the school context in which engagement occurs. This study describes the ecology of involvement and how this social context influences parental involvement and student achievement. Relying on Bronfrenbrenner's theory of human ecology, explains the theoretical model of how the school's social context influences student performance and parental involvement. Analysis using *National Longitudinal Study* that student performance and the relationship between parental involvement and student achievement depends on the ecological context. This finding highlights the need to expand the investigation of parental and child interactions to include aspects of various ecological contexts. This study reveals how parental involvement influences student behavior. Parental involvement, does not occur in a vacuum. There is a particular social context in which parental involvement occurs, contexts that may vary both within and within the school community. Most of the research cited above, and the majority of all studies are parental involvement.

Loke Heng Wang et al (2016), strong parental involvement is one of the factors of school success. Collaboration and partnerships aim to build quality relationships with staff, students, parents, school boards and stakeholders within and outside the school community. Wang's research emphasizes the importance of parental partnership in realizing quality school management performance.

Based on previous studies, it has been known that PAUD is a phase in concept management to realize responsible young people. But from some of these studies nothing has touched the aspect of parental partnership. Discriminant factors are important to study because they reveal the relationship between several factors, especially parental partnership and *good school governance*.

The purpose of this study is to explain the relationship of parental partnership through the factors that cause success in the implementation of *good school governance*. The benefits of this study as material for further research studies that reveal *good school governance,* especially in the scope of early childhood education (PAUD).

https://doi.org/10.1051/matecconf/201820500012

2 Methods

Method in this study is quantitative with a survey approach that reveals the discriminant factors that influence the parent partnership on the success of *good school governance*. This study used a customer satisfaction survey method. Data collection was carried out using questionnaires and interviews to obtain primary data directly from the respondents related to factors that parental partnership that influence the success of *good school governance*.

3 Result and Discussion

This research was conducted between January and October 2017 with respondents covering PAUD throughout Semarang City in Central Java:

3.1 Assumptions Testing for Data Normality

Analysis using structural equation models also requires the distribution of data distribution to meet the assumptions of normality both *univariate* and *multivariate*. Data normality testing used in this study was carried out using the criterion value of the critical ratio (cr) on AMOS output of the skewness value and kurtosis of data distribution. Data is said to have a normal distribution if the critical ratio (cr) value of the skewness and kurtosis values is ± 2,576. Table 1 presents the results of data normality testing in this study.

Table 1. Assessment of Normality

Variable	min	max	skew	cr	kurtosis	cr
Inspire others to move forward with a specific purpose.	30.000	50.000	0.353	20.041	-0.667	-10.925
Having a strategy to move forward	20.000	50.000	0.422	20.434	-0.590	-10.704
Able to communicate well	30.000	50.000	0.404	20.334	-0.747	-20.158
Demonstrate Learning agility,	30.000	50.000	0.159	0.920	-0.527	-10.521
Communication of 2 (two) directions between parents and the school	30.000	50.000	0.315	10.817	-0.885	-20.555
Participate in decisions	30.000	50.000	0.388	20.241	-0.872	-20.517
Have confidence in school	30.000	50.000	0.303	10.750	-0.877	-20.532
active involvement of parents in their children's education activities	30,000	50,000	0.119	0.689	-0.791	-20.284
Scientific	0.664 -0.717 -20.070	50.000	0.115			30.000
Scientific	0.227 10.309 -0.638 -10.841	50.000				30.000
Democratic	10.111 -0.584 -10.686	50.000	0.192			30.000
Cooperative,	-0.509 -10.469	50.000	0.129	0.747		20.000
creative Konstruktifdan	20,000	50,000	0,146	0.843	-0.510	-10.473
Tranparasi	10.876 -0.719 -20.076	50.000	0.325			30.000
Accountability	30.000	50.000	0.263	10.521	-0.728	-20.103
responsibilities	-0.532 -10.535	50.000	0.047	0.271		20.000
Achievement	-0.841 -20.427	50.000	0.132	0.763		20.000
Directed	-0.536 -10.548	50.000	0.161	0.932		20.000
Justice	-0.398 -10.148	50.000	0.087	0.502		30.000
Planning	20.314	50.000	0.401	30.000	-0.829	-20.394

Organizing	20.000	50.000	0.120	0.694	-0.783	- 20.260
Implementation	30.000	50.000	0.091	0.527	-0.756	- 20.183
Supervision	20.000	50.000	0.427	20.464	-0.858	- 20.477
Multivariate					420.458	80.853

Source: the results of the data analysis, 2017

Based *output* on the data with Amospresented in the above table it can be concluded that the distribution of data has met the assumption of normality. This can be seen from the crcoefficients *skewness* and *kurtosis* having a value higher than ± 2,576 (Zα= 00.01 / 2). Likewise cr kurtosis coefficient 80,853 sign thatnormality *multivariate* can be fulfilled because less than 10.

Discriminant validity for constructs of parent partnership and *good school governance* can be calculated by comparing the results of the square root calculation of AVE presented in Table 2 with the magnitude of construct correlation value of parents and *good school governance is* presented in Figure 1.

Table 2. Results ofCalculation Quadratic Rootof AVE Parent Partnership Constructions and Good School Governance

Indicators	Partnershipof parents			*School Good Governance*		
	Std Loading	Std Loading2 Std	Error	Loading	Std Loading2	Error
Communication 2 (two) directions between parents and school parties	0.702	0.493	0.507			
Participating in decision making	0.738	0.545	0.455			
Having confidence in school	0.663	0.440	0.560			
active involvement of parents in their children's education activities	0.703	0.494	0.506			
Scientific	0.676	0.457	0.543			
Tranparasi				0.688	0.473	0.527
Accountability				0.706	0.498	0.502
Responsibility				0.692	0.479	0.521
Achievement				0.690	0.476	0.524
Focus				0.720	0.518	0.482
Justice				0.719	0.517	0.483
Σλ	3.482			4.215		
Σεj		2.43			2.96	
(Σλ) 2 + Σεj			2,57			3,04
Average Variance Extracted (AVE)	0.49			0.49		
Value square root of AVE	0.70			0.70		

Source: Primary data is processed (2017)

While testing the value of the correlation correlation between Parent Partnership with *Good School Governance* obtained RMSCA value of 0.19, CFI value of 996 and DF value of 45.

Table 1 and Figure 1 show that the square root value of AVE for the construct of parent partnership and *good school governance* is greater than the correlation value produced. The square root value of AVE for the parent partnership construct is 0.70 and the square root value of AVE for the construct of *good school governance* is 0.70 and this value is greater than the correlation value between constructs which only produces a value of 0.38. Thus it can be concluded that the indicators of the construct of parental partnership and the *good school governance* studied are completely different and have met the criteria of *discriminant validity*.

3.2 Hypothesis Testing

hypothesis tested is, the better the Parent Partnership, the better the *Good School Governments*. The results of statistical testing of hypothesis 1 using AMOS software as presented in Table 2 shows the standardized estimated parameter values of 0.236; standard error (SE) value of 0.080; the value of critical ratio (CR) is 2.962 with a probability value of 0.003. By using a significance level α = 0.05 it can be concluded that, there is strong empirical evidence to reject Ho and then accept Ha. Thus in this study, the hypothesis which states that the higher parental partnership, the better *good governance schools are* accepted. Utanto et al (2017) states that, "... starting from the preparation of the design model, the development of a model for the learning process and learning output of Web-Based Learning, the preparation of the models and the implementation model to determine the effectiveness of the developed model. "This shows that a model has careful preparation to become a guide in increased relations with other factors. The evidence contained in the processing of this research data shows that the hypothesis obtained is in line with what is said in other relevant research.

Conclusion

As the findings of the study show that the dominant factors are relevant to the success of the program. Strengthened by hypothesis testingwhich shows the results that there is a positive relationship between parental partnership with *good school governance*. The higher the parent's partnership, the better is *good school governance*. So the hypothesis is accepted.

Reference

1. Bungai, J. (2008). "Increasing Equitable Distribution, Quality, Relevance, Governance and Accountability of Park Education".*Journal of Educational Sciences.*15: 74-81.
2. Bredecamp, S. (1987). *Developmentally Appropriate Practice In Early Childhood Program Serving Children From Birth Trough Age 8.*Washington, DC: NAEYC.
3. Director General of PAUDNI, (2013). Technical Guidelines for the Implementation of Pos PAUD, Jakarta.
4. Hanum, Farida and Setya Raharja, (2011). Research Journal of Educational Sciences: Development of Multicultural Education Learning Models. Using Modules as Social Studies Learning Supplements in Primary Schools. Volume 04 No. 2.
5. Ko, J. Cheng, Y. Lee, T., (2016). "The development of school autonomy and accountability in Hong Kong". *International Journal of Educational Management* 30: 1207.
6. Loke Heng Wang, David Gurr, Lawrie Drysdale, (2016). "Successful school leadership: case studies of four Singapore primary schools", Journal of Educational Administration, Vol. 54 Issue: 3, pp.270-287, https://doi.org/10.1108/JEA-03-2015-0022.
7. Permendikbud No. 137 of 2014 concerning PAUD Standards.
8. Ralph B., McNeal Jr., (2014). Parent Involvement, Academic Achievement and the Role of Student Attitudes and Behaviors as Mediators.
9. Siddik, Dja'far, (1984). Basic Concept of Islamic Education. Kudus: Holy Tower.
10. Sumarto. 2009. Increasing Commitment and Satisfaction to Reduce Intention. Exit. Journal of Management and Entrepreneurship, Vol. 11 No. 2, September. 2009, 116-125.
11. Sujiono, Y. Nurani, (2009), Basic Concept of Early Childhood Education, Jakarta: PT Index.
12. Republic of Indonesia Law Number 20 Year 2003, Government Regulation on Early Childhood Education.
13. Utanto, Y., Widhanarto, GP, and Maretta, YA, (2017), March. A Web-based Portfolio Model as the Students Final Assignment: Dealing with the Development of Higher Education Trend. In AIP Conference Proceedings (Vol. 1818, No. 1, p. 020063). AIP Publishing.
14. Republic of Indonesia Law No. 20 of 2003 concerning the National Education System.
15. Wang Ng. Shun, (2013) "Including parents in school governance: rhetoric or reality", International Journal of Educational Management, Vol. 27 Issue: 6, pp.667-680, https://doi.org/10.1108/IJEM-07-2012-0087.

AUTHOR INDEX